Delightfully Free

141 Recipes Free of Gluten, Dairy & Refined Sugar

"Man does not live by bread alone,
but man lives by every word that comes from the mouth of the Lord." Deuteronomy 8:3

Tracy Hill

Photography by Chelsea Armstrong

www.DelightfullyFree.com

The author makes no representations and gives no advice regarding the medical efficacy or appropriateness of any of the recipes or ingredients contained therein. This book does not purport to diagnose or treat any medical condition and the reader should consult with an appropriate medical practitioner before undertaking any alteration in his or her diet or eating habits or those of any consumers of the recipes contained herein. The author disclaims any liability for any adverse effects or consequences resulting from the use of any recipes, information provided or opinions expressed.

Delightfully Free

141 Recipes Free of Gluten, Dairy & Refined Sugar

Delightfully Free Press

Cover Design by Tracy Hill & Chelsea Armstrong

To order this title visit: www.delightfullyfree.com or call (714) 758-5727

Hill, Tracy
Delightfully Free, 2nd Edition, 141 Recipes Free of Gluten, Dairy & Refined Sugar / by Tracy Hill.
p. 176
Includes index
ISBN-10: 978-0-9849383-1-5
2014
Printed in China by Toppan Printing Company Inc.

The joy of writing this book has been, in part, the people who have contributed to make it possible.

From the encouragement to begin, the talents and skills to help put it together, the advice,
and the support and companionship to the last page,
my love and gratitude go to my husband, Brian, my daughter, Chelsea, and Alan.

My heartfelt thanks also to Mom, Sheri, Lori, Christine, Ryan, Aaron and my "testers."

But above all, to God.

Foreword

I have been a clinical nutritionist and homeopathic counselor in Orange County, California since 1999. My scope of clients includes athletes, people who are sick and the person who simply wants to improve health, body composition and energy. I have worked with 5 different physicians in Southern California to help them incorporate clinical nutrition into their practices. Working together, we have found that incorporating clinical nutrition with traditional medicine resolves disease states more quickly, with fewer side effects. I help an individual reach their health goals or resolve their health challenges such as blood sugar issues, food intolerances, celiac disease and other various disease states. I recommend the proper diet and supplements to address their condition. As I explain the need to eliminate foods that are causing these symptoms and the benefit of including some less familiar foods, it has been very difficult to come up with recipes that do so AND that also are appealing and delicious.

Until recently, there were only a few magazines and cookbooks that I could recommend to my clients to assist them in eating this way. Even these included some recipes that were way off track because they contained loads of sugar and other problematic ingredients. Usually, my clients responded by saying that they were willing to make this change in their diet because they needed to, but that their family was going to hate it! They also said that this kind of food "tastes too healthy," meaning bland. Both of these were legitimate complaints. Many of my clients became discouraged after making a couple of meals. Fortunately, the mother of one of my young clients responded by learning all she could about healthy eating and began creating her own unique recipes. Rolling up her sleeves, she has come up with recipes that are both healthy and tasty. No longer is it necessary to cook two meals—one for restricted eaters and one for everyone else. These recipes are so delicious that the whole family will happily eat the same meals. Even those whose diet has not been linked to health issues have so much to benefit from this book. Lean, low in sugar, high in protein and fiber, at the very least the dishes offered in this cookbook will lead to increased muscle, decreased fat, more energy and better mental clarity. I cannot in these few remarks tell you what a gift we have in Tracy's cookbook, but trust you will soon discover it for yourself as you make your way through her varied and creative recipes.

I have tested some of these recipes on my own family. They had no idea they were eating the "clean" kind of foods that I insist on. They actually thought they were getting away with a rare treat. For instance, when I set out a plate of Tracy's chocolate chip cookies, I had to snatch them back before they ate the entire batch. There was no difference in their enthusiasm over Tracy's cookies as compared to traditional chocolate chip cookies with all the white refined four, sugar and other baggage. Tracy and her family have worked tirelessly to give us what I consider a real treasure. I can honestly say that "Delightfully Free" is a blessing. I now have a resource I can recommend to my clients and colleagues. A book that I believe has something for everyone. In recommending some cookbooks in the past, I had to rule out much of their content. But, "Delightfully Free" is compatible with even my own most restrictive plans. Even better, I can now tell my clients that they can still enjoy pasta, saucy entrees, comfort foods, and even desserts. I hope that you will find this cookbook as wonderful as my family and I have. My thanks to Tracy for all her hard work. It has been a pleasure to have had a little input.

Christine Mohler, CN, CHPh.

I Love Good Food and I Especially Love Dessert.

But a number of years ago, I learned that I, and others in my family, had serious food intolerances that knocked out most of our favorite things. Foods like pasta with creamy sauces, pizza, breads, pies and chocolate cake. Living without these for the rest of our lives just wouldn't do. So, I got creative. I experimented. People started saying "Oh! I really want that recipe" and telling me about relatives or friends who couldn't eat dairy or gluten or both. They didn't know what to cook for dinner or any meal for that matter. Many told me I should write a cookbook. Over the past 10 years I have recreated favorite dishes, desserts, muffins and sauces to taste great and at the same time to be healthy. This book contains recipes to make real foods that don't just fill our stomachs but feed our bodies' systems so that they can function the way they were intended to. **All of these recipes are free of gluten, the protein in wheat, casein, the protein in dairy, lactose, refined sugars and yeast. All but one are free of soy.**

In recent years, more people are realizing that there is a real connection between the foods we are eating and the pandemic increase of obesity and disease. The focus has moved beyond the low-calorie, low-fat diet to seeking a level of nutrition that will help address symptoms like problematic digestion, brain fog, low energy, headaches and even aggressive behavior in children, mood swings in adults and inflammation which makes us susceptible to arthritis and disease. We know that medication is not always the answer. Not only are we understanding the dramatic way food affects us, we're discovering that a large part of the equation involves eating gluten-free, dairy-free and free of refined sugars.

In my own experience with family and friends we have seen the dramatic, undeniable effects, both good and bad, caused by what we eat. For example, we have witnessed the most remarkable improvement in aggressive behavior and other autistic symptoms by simply removing gluten, dairy and, in some cases, eggs from the diet of autistic children. This has made the difference between not being able to cope socially and now being able to go to school and be successful. Knowing what to eat, what not to eat and why, has made all the difference.

So many of the people I come across now eat gluten-free, dairy-free or both. Most also recognize the need to lower their intake of sugar. But we still want to eat the delicious foods we love like lasagna, fettuccine with creamy garlic sauce, luscious quiches, moist, flavorful muffins and soft, warm cookies fresh out of the oven. Those packaged ones from the health food stores just don't cut it! What we need is a new version of these foods that is healthy. So, let's compare chocolate chip cookies. When we replace regular chocolate chip cookies with my healthy ones, we have a cookie that will fuel the body instead of wage war against it. The traditional chocolate chip cookie is made of bleached, processed white flour, refined white sugar, refined brown sugar and the unhealthy forms of fat from butter, margarine and shortening (some of which are hydrogenated). Not only are these devoid of any nutritional value, ALL of these ingredients wreck havoc on our bodies.

Happily, my chocolate chip cookies are made of almond meal (100% almonds, a valuable, nutritious food high in protein and fiber), coconut palm sugar (natural and low on the glycemic index and high in nutrients) and grapeseed oil (one of the healthiest, beneficial oils with a very high smoke point). Here, you have a delicious cookie, which is also a nutritious food. Even people who are not "healthy eaters" love them and can't tell that they are gluten-free, dairy-free and free of refined sugar. Another great example is my Black Bean Brownies; their main ingredient is an entire can of black beans. My elegant Chicken de Provence sauce is creamy and rich but it's made out of cauliflower!

Who would have thought that getting a diagnosis that meant being restricted from eating breads, cheese, creamy sauces and rich chocolate desserts would lead to so much good and benefit so many people? But that is what has happened. I believe that even in difficult circumstances, there is a purpose and a blessing. My circumstances led to this cookbook. It's been an adventure to learn a "clean" way of eating by replacing the "foods" we used to eat with real foods that have none of the detrimental, unhealthy baggage.

And now, I want to share this with others. It has been my privilege and pleasure to compile a book of delicious, healthful recipes in a variety of categories from "comfort foods" and family favorites, to foods we thought we would never be able to eat again, and even more elegant, festive dishes. My hope is that this collection, along with my blog at www.delightfullyfree.com, will help you and your family to improve and preserve your health and quality of life while enjoying the foods you love for the seasons you celebrate. Let's put the joy back into cooking and eating, free of the stuff that makes us sick...

Delightfully Free!

What's New in This Second Edition

The first printing of Delightfully Free was met with enthusiasm beyond what I could have imagined. I have had the privilege and pleasure of meeting hundreds of health practitioners (most of whom now carry the book as a resource for their patients), as well as thousands of very knowledgeable natural food retailers and consumers. Over the course of these discussions and exchanges of ideas, I noticed a growing consensus that better choices are now available for low-glycemic natural sweeteners than agave nectar.

Because my goal is to create new recipes and recreate old favorites in the most delicious and healthy way possible, I decided to rework just over 50 recipes to eliminate agave nectar. I did this in most cases by increasing the measure of coconut palm sugar and/or stevia. In more limited instances, I added coconut nectar, and in a few recipes, raw honey. Because they are new to the book and may be unfamiliar to some, coconut nectar and raw honey have been added to "Stocking Your GF, DF, SF Pantry"--a section I highly recommend reading for the very best results. In the process, I feel that improvements have been made all the way around. I am delighted to say that these reworked recipes are even more delicious and more healthy than before. I hope you'll agree!

Wishing you health and Joy,
Tracy

Stocking Your GF, DF, SF Pantry

There are a number of ingredients that make this kind of cooking and baking possible. Each one adds an important characteristic to the finished product. Even if they sound foreign to start with, once you have stocked them in your pantry, it all seems simpler. Many of them (like xanthan gum) will last for a very long time because you only need to use a small amount in each recipe (½ to 1 tsp in the case of xanthan gum). Others you will purchase repeatedly because they are your new friends and allow you to eat the things you have been missing.

You don't need to purchase them all at once. Start with the ingredients you need this week for the recipes you have chosen to make. If you're going to bake, you'll probably need a couple of flours, natural sweeteners and some xanthan gum. All of the ingredients in this book can be found easily in most local health food or natural food markets, including the ones that carry Delightfully Free. For a list of locations that sell Delightfully Free in your area, please visit my website, www.delightfullyfree.com. The ingredients can also be purchased online. Here are some of the key ingredients which are staples in a GF, DF, SF kitchen. Most, if not all, of these ingredients come organic.

Low-Glycemic, Natural Sweeteners

In this book I have used a combination of only three unrefined, low-glycemic natural sweeteners. They are stevia, coconut palm sugar (in granular and syrup form) and in seven recipes, raw honey. For diabetics and others who must limit their sugar even more, I recommend using the stevia with the other sweeteners as directed by your doctor or nutritionist.

COCONUT PALM SUGAR is a granular, natural, unrefined sweetener made from the flower of the coconut palm tree. It has fewer calories than honey or agave nectar. Not only does coconut palm sugar have a low glycemic index of about 35 compared to table sugar with a glycemic index of 80, it is actually a nutrient-rich food containing key vitamins, minerals and phytonutrients. It has a rich flavor, which is considered to be preferable to white or brown sugar. In cooking and baking, it behaves much like traditional sugar, and so allows for easy substitution and the same desired results.

COCONUT NECTAR is a sweet syrup which, like coconut palm sugar, is the unprocessed "sap" of the coconut tree blossom. Although they come from the coconut tree, they do not have a coconut flavor. Like coconut palm sugar, coconut nectar is nutrient-dense, containing 17 amino acids, vitamin C, broad-spectrum B vitamins and a neutral pH. Both the granular and the syrup have a low-glycemic index of 35, are raw, unprocessed, high in nutrients and have a delicious flavor, making them superior to other "natural" sweeteners.

STEVIA is an all natural, plant-derived sweetener which comes in liquid or powder form. It is intensely sweet, 200-300 times more than table sugar, although it is not a sugar. Stevia has no calories and a glycemic index of zero. Because it can have a bitter aftertaste, I use it in combination with coconut palm sugar and coconut nectar to cut down even the amount of natural sugars in my recipes. It is important to measure stevia accurately because it can overpower and ruin the dish.

RAW HONEY In the few instances where honey is called for, always use **raw** which is preferable for a variety of reasons. Most important for our purposes is that it is unprocessed and scores between 30-40 on the glycemic index compared to processed honeys which score between 55-80.

Flours

There are many GF flours and meals. I have listed only the ones used in this book. I recommend keeping them in sealed containers and refrigerated or frozen for freshness.

ARROWROOT FLOUR (also called arrowroot starch or powder) is a pure starch which is ground from the root of the arrowroot plant. It is a very light-weight, tasteless, white powder which works well to thicken liquids (other than dairy) without making them cloudy so it is especially useful when making a clear glaze or fruit sauce. In baking, arrowroot flour lightens and softens the texture of breads, cakes or muffins that would otherwise be denser. It also acts as a binding agent.

BROWN RICE FLOUR (different from white rice flour, which I don't use) is made from unrefined, unpolished brown rice so it has a higher nutritional value and does not turn to sugar rapidly like white rice. It still contains the bran of the rice, so it also has a higher fiber content. It has a slightly nutty taste and because its texture is a bit grainy, it produces a heavier composition in baked goods. It works well in muffins, cookies and crumbles. It can add crispiness and so is the main ingredient in my Basic Pie Crust.

COCONUT FLOUR is one of the most healthy flours because it is made purely of ground coconut meat, consisting of 58% dietary fiber and is very high in protein. It contains fewer carbs than other flours and most of the carbs it does have are non-digestible carbs which have no calories. Ideal for baking, coconut flour has a natural, sweet flavor and produces a moist crumb, enhancing the flavor and texture of baked goods.

GARBANZO BEAN FLOUR is roasted, finely ground garbanzo beans (or chickpeas). Since it is 100% a bean/pea, it is packed with protein & fiber, a good source of iron and low in fat. This makes it a great meatless source of protein. It does have a strong flavor which lessens after baking, so is best used in combination with other flours.

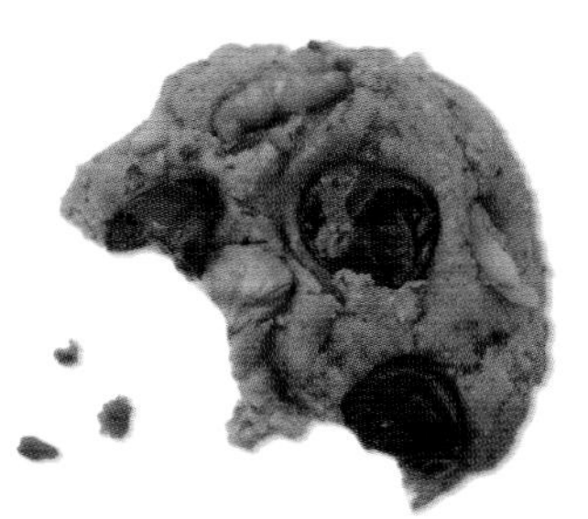

POTATO STARCH is different from potato flour. It is made from only the starch of the potato (while potato flour is made from the whole potato). An alternative to corn starch, it is used to thicken sauces, soups and gravies. In baking, it adds moistness, creates structure and works as a binding agent. Unlike other GF flours, potato starch has very little nutritional value.

SORGHUM FLOUR is a mild, sweet, finely ground flour made from whole sorghum grain. It is very versatile in baking and works in almost any recipe including pancakes, muffins and cookies. If used alone, it produces a drier, more crumbly texture without chewiness. When combined with tapioca flour or brown rice flour, for example, it improves texture and creates a fine crumb. I also use it in my roux for sauces.

TAPIOCA FLOUR is made from the root of the cassava plant. Ground into a velvety, soft, white powder, it is slightly sweet. It is a good thickener in cooking, and in baking it lightens and creates a texture that is more like those baked with wheat flour. It adds chewiness, and so is a perfect choice to use in pizza crust.

Meals & Grains

ALMOND MEAL is simply ground almonds, which are a nutritious, whole food packed with protein, vitamin E, monounsaturated (good) fats, minerals, calcium and fiber. Using almond meal is a wonderful way to bring high amounts of protein and fiber to baked goods which are completely missing in traditional baking. It creates a moist crumb and allows a better rise in baked goods. Almond meal can replace dry milk powder in most recipes and is relatively inexpensive.

AMARANTH is the tiny seed of the amaranth plant, even smaller than quinoa. It is a nutritious whole grain, used interchangeably with rice, pasta, couscous or quinoa. It is high in protein and contains 2 times as much calcium as cow's milk and 3 times more fiber than wheat.

BUCKWHEAT (BUCKWHEAT GROATS OR KERNELS), despite its name, is not related to wheat and is actually GF. Although it is usually referred to as a cereal grain, it is a type of fruit, related to the rhubarb plant. It is high in magnesium with 4g fiber, 10g protein and 0g sugar per 1/2 cup. It gives a wonderful crunch to cookies and pie crusts and is also ground into flour for baking.

FLAXSEED MEAL (ground flaxseeds) is nutrient dense (having more omega 3 than salmon), high in fiber, protein, vitamins and minerals. It adds a nutty flavor and a chewy texture to cooking and baking. It can be used as an egg substitute by simmering 1 Tbsp in 3 Tbsp of water = 1 egg, or a fat substitute, 2 Tbsp flaxseed meal = 1 Tbsp butter or oil.

MILLET is technically a seed but is usually classified as a nutritious grain because of its grain-like consistency. It is tiny and round, with a neutral flavor, so it can be added to a variety of dishes. It is high in protein (right behind quinoa), phosphorus, manganese, magnesium and other important nutrients.

GF STEEL CUT OATS are the only type I use because they are a whole grain--unrefined, still natural, and so much healthier. Rolled oats, which are used in most recipes, are steamed, flattened, re-steamed and toasted. Consequently, they share the same big problem that all processed foods have. Not only have they lost most of their nutrition and fiber, they now break down rapidly and turn to sugar, but steel cut oats, on the other hand, provide a constant, steady fuel of protein, nutrients and fiber which keeps blood sugar in check.

GF OAT BRAN is the outer husk of the oat grain. It is unfortunately usually discarded in the processing of rolled oats and other oat products. It is very low in cholesterol and sodium but packed with protein, fiber, iron and a long list of minerals and other important nutrients. It is a health food, even considered to be a nutritional supplement. I use it extensively in my muffin and pancake recipes because it is a fabulous way to incorporate loads of nutrition, bakes beautifully, and produces delicious results.

QUINOA (pronounced 'keen wa') is actually a seed and is a complete protein source with all 8 essential amino acids, higher in protein than any comparable grain (5.5 grams per 1 cup cooked). It is also a great source of fiber and other nutrients. It makes an interesting alternative to rice or couscous. Quinoa flakes are simply a cereal made from quinoa.

Unusual Ingredients

AGAR is a natural vegetable gelatin which can be used instead of the unflavored gelatin, such as Knox® gelatin, commonly used in Jello® and other aspics. It is derived from the jelly of various species of seaweed. The ratio of agar to the liquid used is different than that of traditional gelatin, so it must be carefully substituted. Another vegetarian option is Veg-a-gel®.

ALMOND AND RICE MILKS are the two dairy-free milk alternatives used in my recipes along with coconut milk. They work very well in DF cooking and baking, enabling us to create creamy sauces, fluffier egg dishes and the same results cows' milk produces in baking. Almond milk, made from almonds, naturally contains far more nutrients at higher levels than rice milk, made from brown rice. Preference of taste and compatibility with the recipe dictate which is the best choice. They come in "Plain" or "Vanilla" flavor. Note that in almost every recipe in my book, I use "Plain."

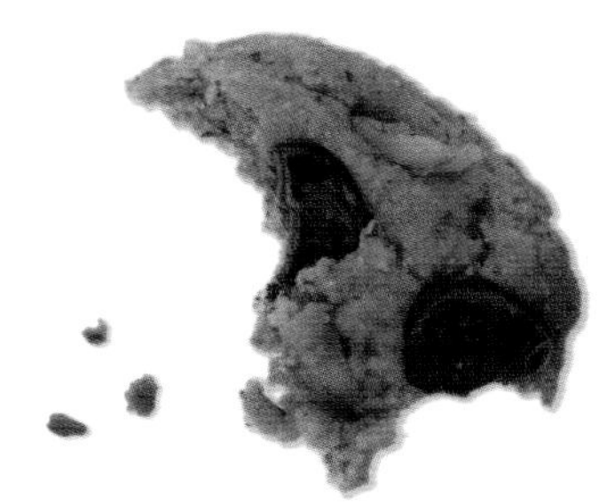

ORGANIC DF, LESS-SWEETENED DARK CHOCOLATE is what I use in my recipes that call for chocolate chips and chocolate chunks. There are several brands to choose from which do not include gluten or dairy products in their list of ingredients, although some use equipment which is shared in the production of dairy products. Some brands come in the form of chocolate chips but others are available only in bar form. These we cut into pieces on a cutting board using the point of a knife. Depending on your emphasis, some of the chocolate options include:

- Chocolate Dream® Semi-Sweet Baking Chips
- Endangered Species® All-Natural Dark Chocolate Bars
- Enjoy Life® Semi-Sweet Mini Chips
- Equal Exchange® Organic Very Dark Chocolate Bars
- Scharffen Berger Chocolates
- Sunspire® Organic Bittersweet Chocolate Chips

COCONUT MILK is not the liquid found in the middle of the coconut. It is the juice expressed from the meat of the coconut. One cup contains 38.4mg calcium, about 89mg magnesium, 631mg potassium and 240mg phosphorus. It also is a great source of manganese, copper and zinc. It lends a creamy, rich flavor which is fabulous for DF cooking. In each recipe that calls for coconut milk, it means **canned coconut milk**, not the beverage. Be sure to note whether it is "light" or "whole" coconut milk called for in the recipe, and stir it well before measuring.

COCONUT OIL is the fatty oil that comes from coconut meat. Quality, raw, organic coconut oil is a good choice for cooking, frying and baking because it is heat stable, which makes it slow to oxidize and resistant to becoming rancid. It has a pleasant, mild coconut flavor which becomes a delicious bonus in some recipes and is undetected in others.

GRAPESEED OIL is what I generally use to "grease" the baking dishes and cook with on high heats because of its neutral flavor, affordability, and high smoke point of 420° F. The smoke point of an oil is the temperature at which it breaks down chemically into harmful toxins including free radicals.

100% CRISPY BROWN RICE is an unsweetened crispy rice cereal. It can be purchased in some health food stores in bulk. If you can't find it unsweetened, Barbara's® makes a version sweetened only with fruit juice.

EGG REPLACERS are a wonderful option for vegans and those with egg sensitivities. Four egg replacer options are: flaxseed meal (in this lexicon, p.5), ground chia seeds (1 Tbsp ground chia seeds soaked in 3 Tbsp water 5-6 minutes = 1 egg), 1/4 cup silken puréed tofu plus 1 tsp baking powder = 1 egg (not always applicable in baking), and powdered egg replacers. Ener-G® brand is a reliable choice. I have found that the results are far better if the mixture of the powder and water is whisked and allowed to sit for at least 10 minutes. Replacing more than 2 eggs will change the consistency of a recipe. For recipes that use more eggs, you will need to adjust by slightly lowering other liquid ingredients and possibly increasing the baking time.

GHEE is clarified butter. Although butter is a dairy product, ghee no longer contains any casein (the protein in dairy) or lactose. It is concentrated, so a little ghee provides a buttery flavor in DF cooking.

GOLD POTATOES, such as Yukon Gold, are a better choice than white potatoes because of the way they are used by the body. They have a yellow-colored flesh containing vitamin A and antioxidants, and are rich in potassium. They are much healthier than white potatoes because once eaten, the carbohydrates of white potatoes are very quickly converted to sugar, while gold potatoes break down more slowly, not spiking blood sugar. When cooked, they have a creamy texture and a buttery flavor.

ORGANIC NON-HYDROGENATED VEGETABLE SHORTENING is different from the old shortening our mothers used. Even though some of the old brands have been reformulated in recent years to be 100% vegetable derived, their processing includes hydrogenation, which is harmful for the body to ingest. They even include small amounts of trans fats. Spectrum® brand is organic, all vegetable, non-hydrogenated and kosher.

SEA SALT is healthier than table salt but has a less salty flavor, so it is important to use sea salt instead of regular salt in these recipes or you will not have the same result.

XANTHAN GUM is one of the most important ingredients in GF baking. Gluten, the protein in wheat, is what binds baked goods together and gives them their elastic, spongy quality. Xanthan gum provides this essential element in GF baking. It also thickens liquids such as salad dressings and sauces. Even though an 8 ounce bag costs just over $10, it goes a long way because it is used in very small amounts, ½ to 1 tsp in most recipes. The corn sensitive person should use a corn-free xanthan gum such as Bob's Red Mill® or substitute with guar gum.

Tips

Every recipe in this book has been carefully thought out. Unlike traditional cooking, GF cooking, and especially baking, requires the ingredients to be measured correctly or else it really throws off the results. GF doughs are sometimes thinner, looking more like a batter. Crust doughs vary as well. Trust the recipe. The key to successful GF baking is to **follow the directions exactly and measure the ingredients precisely** using the straight edge of a knife to level each teaspoon, tablespoon and measuring cup.

There is a difference between wet and dry measuring cups. For accurate measurement of ingredients, use a wet measuring cup which has a spout for all ingredients that drip like oil, coconut nectar and coconut milk. Use a dry measuring cup which has a flat top for dry ingredients like flours, oats, beans, lentils and chopped vegetables in order to use the straight edge of a knife to level off the top.

You will save a lot of time and frustration by reading the whole recipe before starting. This way, you will have ingredients like vegetables peeled, chopped and ready to be added at the right moment instead of delaying time-sensitive steps and changing the end result. In addition to reading the recipe all the way through before starting, be sure to follow the recipe exactly. Attention to detail in GF, DF, SF cooking and baking produces the best results.

Other Tools You Will Need

A good blender or food processor is essential for the cakes, frostings, pies, mousses, soups, sauces and egg dishes as well as many other recipes in this book. I find that a blender works very well for all of these purposes. Using a blender or food processor often makes a recipe quick and simple! An immersion blender is even better for certain recipes like the cakes and brownies.

A silicone spatula saves so much time and is vastly more efficient at getting the batter, frosting, soup, etc. out of the blender and even the mixing bowls.

Parchment paper is necessary for lining the bottom of cake pans.

An oil mister is great and economical for spraying baking pans and dishes and the saute pans. Also, a mister is best for preparing the tortillas in several of the recipes.

In addition to the typical measuring spoons, a 1/16,⅛, ⅓ and 1½ tsp (which = ½ Tbsp) measures are very helpful and will save you time.

A wire mesh strainer is necessary for straining the soaked oats, draining beans, rinsing grains and even works as a substitute for a flour sifter if you don't have one.

A small and a large wire whisk are needed for whisking eggs and sauces, and also for whisking flours and other dry ingredients together, blending and separating them much like a sifter.

Metric Conversions

Common Liquid Measurements

⅛ tsp	=	0.625 milliliters
¼ tsp	=	1.25 ml
½ tsp	=	2.50 ml
⅔ tsp	=	3.30 ml
¾ tsp	=	3.75 ml
1 tsp	=	5.00 ml
1¼ tsp	=	6.25 ml
1½ tsp	=	7.50 ml
1¾ tsp	=	8.75 ml
2 tsp	=	10.00 ml
1 Tbsp	=	15.00 ml
2 Tbsp	=	30.00 ml

¼ cup	=	.06 liters
½ cup	=	.12 l
⅔ cup	=	.15 l
¾ cup	=	.18 l
1 cup	=	.24 l
1¼ cups	=	.30 l
1½ cups	=	.36 l
1⅔ cups	=	.40 l
2 cups	=	.48 l
2½ cups	=	.60 l
2⅔ cups	=	.64 l
3 cups	=	.72 l
3½ cups	=	.84 l
4 cups	=	.96 l

English to Metric Formulas

tsp	x	5.0	=	milliliters
Tbsp	x	15.0	=	milliliters
fluid oz	x	30.0	=	milliliters

Weight

cups	x	0.24	=	liters
oz	x	28.00	=	grams
pounds	x	0.45	=	kilograms

Temperatures

275° F	=	140° C	gas mark 1-cool
300° F	=	150° C	gas mark 2
325° F	=	165° C	gas mark 3-very moderate
350° F	=	180° C	gas mark 4-moderate
375° F	=	190° C	gas mark 5
400° F	=	200° C	gas mark 6-moderately hot
425° F	=	220° C	gas mark 7-hot
450° F	=	230° C	gas mark 9
475° F	=	240° C	gas mark 10-very hot

Soaking Steel Cut Oats for Baking

Dry Oats	Salt	Coconut Palm Sugar	Water	Yield
1½ cups	½ tsp	¼ cup	3 cups	2⅓ cups
2 cups	¾ tsp	⅓ cup	4 cups	3 cups
2½ cups	¾ tsp	½ cup	5 cups	3½ cups
3 cups	1 tsp	½ cup	5 cups	4½ cups

To prepare steel cut oats to be used for baking, they must be softened and opened up. To do this, soak them in water overnight or for at least 10 hours. It is simple to do but requires a little planning.

Use GF steel cut oats. If desired, chop oats briefly in a food processor or food chopper to create a finer texture in the finished baked product.

Mix desired amount of oats in a bowl with salt, sugar and water, cover and soak 10 or more hours in the refrigerator.

Use a wire strainer, working with 2 cups of oats at a time, press the water out with the bottom of a small bowl that fits into the strainer. Next, dump the oats out onto 2 thicknesses of paper toweling. Fold the towels over the oats and press any remaining water out. Repeat with the rest of the soaked oats.

Now, the oats are ready to be used in recipes for baking. Store in the refrigerator.

Baking Soaked Steel Cut Oats

Preheat oven to 275°. Brush or spray a jelly roll pan with grapeseed oil. Spread the soaked, drained oats out evenly on the pan and bake 1 hour. Allow to cool completely on the pan. They will continue to become crispy as they cool. Loosen with a spatula.

Main Dishes

Chicken Enchilada Casserole

Serves 6-8 Veg & V*, Egg Free, Corn Free

6 9" brown rice tortillas, such as Trader Joe's® or Food for Life®

Sauce

- 46 oz chicken stock or broth
- 3 Tbsp dehydrated minced onion**
- ¼ cup chili powder
- 2 tsp garlic powder
- ¼ tsp cumin
- 1¾ tsp sea salt
- 3½ Tbsp unsweetened cocoa powder
- 4 Tbsp tapioca flour stirred in 3 Tbsp water

A fiesta of flavor, these enchiladas are so creamy and satisfying! I've been enthusiastically told, "I didn't even miss the cheese, and I'm a cheese person!" To jazz it up further, add a 4 oz can of diced green chiles to the filling.

Filling

- 2 cups cooked lentils
- 4 boneless, skinless chicken breasts about 2¼ lbs
- ¾ cup plain hummus, p.123
- ¾ cup black olives, sliced
- ¾ cup green onions, sliced
- 4 oz can diced green chiles, optional

Garnish

- ½ cup olives, sliced
- ½ cup green onions, sliced

Preheat oven to 350°. Sprinkle chicken breasts with sea salt and garlic powder, place in a baking dish and bake uncovered 20 minutes, just until centers are no longer pink. Shred chicken, cover and set aside. In a 4-qt pot, whisk together the chicken stock, dehydrated onion, chili powder, garlic powder, cumin, salt and unsweetened cocoa. Heat to a simmer, stirring constantly. Whisk in tapioca-water mixture and cook 1 minute as you stir. Turn off heat. Pour ¾ cup of sauce into shredded chicken and mix well.

Spray or brush a 9x13 baking dish with grapeseed oil. Spoon just enough sauce into the dish to cover bottom. Dip 2 tortillas into the pot of sauce and lay them in the dish, covering the bottom. Trim excess tortilla from edges and reserve. Spread ½ of the chicken over tortillas, then ½ of the lentils. Using ½ of the hummus, drop dollops over lentils. Sprinkle with ½ of the olives and green onions. Spoon a generous amount of sauce evenly over top, and repeat the steps to create a next layer. Patch any spaces in tortilla layer needing to be filled using reserved scraps from dipped tortillas. End with last 2 tortillas on top and cover with sauce. Remaining sauce can be served with enchiladas at the table. Bake uncovered 30-40 minutes or until heated through and beginning to bubble around the edges. Garnish with remaining olives and green onions. Allow to set for 8-10 minutes before serving.

*Note: For vegetarian/vegan option, eliminate the chicken and use vegetable broth instead of chicken broth.

**Dehydrated onion lends a desired effect, so don't substitute with fresh.

Chipotle Meatballs

Makes 28-30 Egg Free (substitute oil), Corn Free

- 1 cup yellow onion, minced
- 1½ Tbsp seeded Serrano chile, minced, optional for more heat
- 3 large cloves garlic, minced
- 1½ Tbsp olive oil
- 1 lb ground turkey
- 1 small egg, or 1 Tbsp olive oil
- ¼ cup + 1 Tbsp brown rice flour
- 1¾ tsp sea salt
- 2¼ tsp moderately hot fire-roasted chipotle powder
- ½ tsp GF liquid smoke, such as Wright's®
- 2 Tbsp coconut palm sugar

These meatballs are savory and satisfying as a main course served with a side dish like Kale & Onions on p.107. They are also delicious in the Chipotle Meatballs with Peppers & Onions, p.23, or in the Chipotle Meatball soup recipe on p.89.

In a medium skillet, cook the onion and minced chile, if using, in olive oil on medium heat about 6 minutes or until onions are softened. Add the garlic and cook 1 minute. Set aside. Preheat oven to 350°. Brush or spray a baking sheet with grapeseed oil. In a large bowl (I use glass or metal when working with raw meat), mix ground turkey with egg using a large, sturdy spoon. Add remaining ingredients and mix thoroughly. Form 1½ inch meatballs on baking sheet. Bake 18-20 minutes, just until centers are no longer pink.

Italian Meatballs

Makes 45 Egg Free (substitute oil), Corn Free

- ½ lb ground turkey
- 1 lb uncooked sweet Italian chicken sausage, casings removed
- 1 small egg, or 1 Tbsp olive oil
- ¼ cup fresh basil, chopped, or 1½ tsp dried
- 1 tsp dried fennel seed
- ¾ tsp sea salt
- ¾-1 cup brown rice breadcrumbs, depending on consistency

Serve with my Old World Tomato Basil Marinara and gluten-free pasta, or in a soup to give it an Italian flair, or on my Quick Bread, or other gluten-free bread as a meatball sandwich. This recipe makes 45 meatballs. You can freeze half to bring out later on a busy day.

Preheat oven to 350°. Brush or spray a baking sheet with grapeseed oil. In a large bowl (I use glass or metal when mixing raw meat), mix the ground turkey with sausage meat using a large, sturdy spoon. Add the egg and seasonings, and mix well. Stir in ¾ cup of the breadcrumbs. If the mixture is too wet, add a little more breadcrumbs. Form 1½ inch meatballs on the baking sheet. Bake 20 minutes, just until the centers of the meatballs are no longer pink. Do not overcook. Pat dry with a paper towel.

Corn-Free Crispy Taco Shells

Makes 4 Taco Shells Veg, V, Egg Free, Corn Free

- 4 9" brown rice tortillas, such as Trader Joe's® or Food for Life® (shells will be about twice average size)
- 1 tsp olive oil (¼ tsp for each tortilla. An oil mister is recommended)
- • sea salt
- 3 unshelled walnuts for each tortilla (The walnuts may be re-used indefinitely)

Preheat oven to 350°. Lay tortillas on a baking sheet, edges may touch but should not overlap. I recommend making no more than 4 at a time. Spray both sides of each tortilla very lightly with an oil mister, then use a pastry brush to spread oil evenly. Sprinkle both sides of each tortilla lightly with sea salt and bake 3 minutes. Remove from oven and carefully place 3 walnuts on each tortilla. Fold it in half, using the walnuts to support the upper half, forming the shape of the shell. Bake 4 minutes, flip each shell over and bake an additional 4 minutes, creating an even golden brown. Remove from oven and remove walnuts immediately.

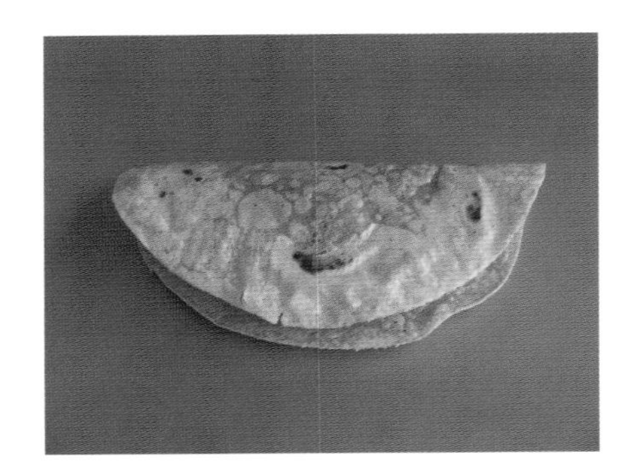

Vegetarian Bean Taco Filling

Makes 4-5 Tacos   Veg, V, Egg Free, Corn Free

- 1 15 oz can black beans, drained
- 1 15 oz can pinto beans, drained
- ¾ cup water
- ¼ cup dehydrated minced onion*
- 1 large clove garlic, minced, or ¾ tsp garlic powder
- 2½ Tbsp chile powder, or to taste
- ¼ tsp dried oregano
- ¾ cup walnuts
- 1 tsp sea salt
- ¾ tsp cumin
- 1-2 Tbsp grapeseed oil

"Check the label." This needs to be our mantra. Often, foods we would not expect to contain gluten or casein, do. This is true of many packaged and prepared foods. Gluten and casein are hidden in products like soups, sauces, salad dressings, and soy sauce, and in ingredients like some baking powders and baking yeasts, malt, maltodextrin, modified food starch, hydrolyzed vegetable protein (HVP), and most taco seasoning mixes, to name a few.

In a blender or food processor, pulse the walnuts 3-5 times until coarsely chopped. Combine the beans in a mixing bowl and mash half with a potato masher or wooden spoon, leaving remainder unmashed. Stir together the water and dehydrated onion in a skillet and cook on medium heat 1-2 minutes, until onion is softened. Pour water and onion into bean mixture. Stir in walnuts and all remaining ingredients, except oil. Mix thoroughly. Coat bottom of skillet with oil. Cook bean mixture on medium heat, stirring constantly until heated. Spoon into shells and enjoy.

Turkey Taco Filling

Makes 4-5 Tacos   Egg Free, Corn Free

- 1 Tbsp grapeseed oil
- 1 lb ground turkey
- 1 large clove garlic, minced, or ¾ tsp garlic powder
- ¼ cup dehydrated minced onion*
- 2 Tbsp chile powder
- 1 tsp sea salt
- ½ tsp cumin

Yum! Crispy, light and so much fun to eat—for kids too. They are quick and easy to make. To best prepare these taco shells, I recommend using a mister, such as a Misto®. A mister spreads the oil much more sparingly than a brush does. After spraying it on, spread it using a brush for best results.

In a skillet, cook the turkey in the oil on medium-high heat, stirring often to break it up and cook it evenly. Cover when not stirring. Cook 8-10 minutes, until the meat is no longer pink. Drain any fat. Stir in remaining ingredients. Add a couple Tbsp of water if mixture is too dry. Cook covered on low heat 3-4 minutes, stirring occasionally until heated through. Spoon into taco shells and enjoy.

Top either taco filling with any of your favorites...

Diced tomatoes	Chopped onion	Sliced black olives	GF salsa or taco sauce
Shredded lettuce	Any diced chile	Avocados/guacamole	Fresh cilantro

*Note: Dehydrated onion lends a certain desired effect, so don't substitute with fresh.

Black Bean Veggie Burgers

Makes 4 Burgers — Veg, V & Egg Free (w/ egg replacer), Corn Free

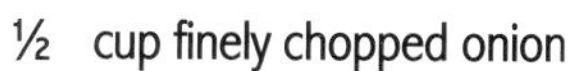

- ½ cup finely chopped onion
- ¼ cup shredded zucchini
- ¼ cup shredded carrot
- ¼ cup finely chopped yellow or red bell pepper
- ¼ cup finely chopped crimini mushrooms
- 1 15 oz can black beans, rinsed well using a strainer and drained on a paper towel
- 1 large egg
- 3 large cloves garlic, minced using a garlic press
- 1⅛ tsp sea salt
- ⅛ tsp cayenne pepper
- ½ tsp cumin
- 1 tsp chili powder
- ½ cup GF bread crumbs

The recipe for these burger rolls is on p.57.

A great way to eat a high-fiber, protein-packed, low-fat, vegetable-rich meal that is full of exciting flavor. Crumble leftovers over a salad or stir into scrambled eggs.

Chop, shred and measure out each of the 5 vegetables into a bowl and set aside. In another bowl, mash most of the black beans with a large fork or potato masher and set aside. In a large bowl, whisk the egg. Add the garlic, salt, cayenne pepper, cumin and chili powder, and whisk again until well combined. Spoon beans into the egg mixture. Add the breadcrumbs and veggies, and mix well. Brush a griddle with grapeseed oil and warm over medium heat. Form the patties and cook 6-7 minutes on each side until they turn golden brown. These patties are very delicate, so flip them carefully. Remove from heat and enjoy with or without buns.

Turkey Burgers

Makes 5-6 Burgers — Egg Free (substitute oil), Corn Free

- 1 lb ground turkey
- 1 small egg, or 1 Tbsp olive oil
- ¼ cup brown rice flour
- ¼ tsp garlic powder
- 1⅛ tsp sea salt
- ¼ tsp black pepper

Be sure to try these burgers with the homemade rolls on p.57. And if you haven't yet had yam fries, you absolutely must try the Baked Yam Fries, p.105. This dinner is one of our family's summer favorites.

In a glass or metal mixing bowl, combine all ingredients and mix well. Preheat grill, adjust heat to medium-low and brush or spray generously with grapeseed oil. Or, if you prefer, heat a skillet that has been brushed with grapeseed oil. Form patties about 3½-4" wide by ¾" thick on a sheet of waxed paper. I cut the paper into squares around the patties, leaving each patty on its own square of paper; this way, it's easier to place them on the grill by holding each patty by its paper and quickly setting it meat side down onto the grill. Remove paper and cook 4-5 minutes. Gently work a metal spatula under patties to flip them. Grill another 4-5 minutes, until no longer pink in center. If using a skillet, place patties on skillet and cook according to the directions for the grill.

Stuffed Bell Peppers

Serves 6 Egg Free, Corn Free

- 6 green bell peppers with flat bottoms
- 1 Tbsp olive oil
- 1 lb ground turkey
- 2 cups chopped onion
- 2-3 cloves garlic, minced
- 1¼ tsp sea salt
- 2 tsp fresh oregano leaves, or ½ tsp dried
- 1 15 oz can tomato sauce
- 1½ cups cooked brown rice

Garnish

- 1 8 oz can (or 1 cup) tomato sauce
- Additional oregano to garnish

This recipe definitely falls under the category of "home-cooked comfort foods." They look impressive on the plate, taste wonderful, are filling and satisfying and, at the same time, are completely nutritious, GF, DF and SF!

Wash peppers, uniformly cut off the tops and remove seeds. Bring a large pot of water to a boil. Cook peppers 3 at a time in boiling water for 3-4 minutes or until they begin to soften. Don't overcook; peppers will continue to soften in oven. Use tongs or a slotted spoon to remove peppers and drain upside down on a paper towel. Preheat oven to 350°. Spray a baking dish sized to fit the peppers with grapeseed oil. Meanwhile, in a skillet, brown the ground turkey and onion in olive oil on medium-high heat 7-8 minutes until cooked. Drain, return to heat and stir in the garlic, salt, oregano, the 15 oz tomato sauce, and rice. Set peppers into baking dish and fill each with meat/rice mixture. Bake uncovered 10-12 minutes. Spoon tomato sauce over each stuffed pepper and sprinkle with oregano.

Dixie Party Meatloaf

Serves 8-10 Egg Free, Corn Free

- 2 lb ground turkey
- ¾ cup onion, chopped
- 1 cup red, orange or yellow bell pepper, chopped
- ¾ tsp dried oregano leaves
- 1 6 oz can tomato paste
- ¾ tsp garlic powder
- 2 tsp sea salt
- 2 Tbsp fresh parsley, chopped
- 1 Tbsp grapeseed oil
- ½ cup brown rice flour

This meatloaf is moist and flavorful, and large enough for a whole party. It's quick and easy to make, and always a crowd-pleaser. If you have any left over, it's delicious served sliced over a salad with my Creamy Mustard Dressing, p.102, or as a meatloaf sandwich using the Seeded Quick Bread, p.59.

Preheat oven to 350°. Brush the bottom of a 9x13 casserole or roasting pan with grapeseed oil. In a large bowl (preferably glass or metal when working with raw meat), mix all ingredients with a large, sturdy spoon. Turn onto casserole or pan, and form into a loaf. Bake uncovered 40-50 minutes until center is no longer pink.

Lentil Stew

Serves 6 — Veg, V, Egg Free, Corn Free

- 1 medium eggplant, about 1½ lb
- 2 Tbsp olive oil, plus a little more
- • garlic powder
- 1 medium yellow onion, 2 cups chopped
- 1 serrano chile pepper, stemmed, seeded & chopped, or more to taste
- 3 cloves garlic, minced
- 1 Tbsp cumin
- 1 tsp chili powder
- 1 tsp turmeric
- ½ tsp dried oregano
- 1 15 oz can garbanzo beans, drained
- 1 cup dried lentils
- 1 28 oz can tomato puree
- 2 cups vegetable broth or 1 14½ oz can + 1½ oz water
- 1 tsp sea salt

"Variety is the spice of life." This stew is deliciously different. Hearty and savory, bursting with the goodness of legumes, and, at only 250 calories per serving, it packs 17g protein and nearly 5g fiber at just under 5g fat. Try it with the Cornbread or Harvest Pumpkin Bread.

Preheat oven to 400° and brush or spray a roasting pan with grapeseed oil. Cut eggplant in slices approximately 1" thick and brush with olive oil. Sprinkle with sea salt and garlic powder and roast in oven 8 minutes. Remove, cool and cut into ½" pieces. The skin can be stripped off easily, if desired. Meanwhile, in a skillet, saute the onions in 2 Tbsp of oil 8 minutes. Add the serrano pepper and garlic, and cook 2 minutes until peppers begin to soften. Combine everything in a slow cooker and cook on high 3 hours, or up to 8 hours on low; or if desired, in a pot on low heat, stirring occasionally 1½ hours.

Chipotle Meatballs with Peppers & Onions

Serves 5-6 — Egg Free

- 24 chipotle meatballs, recipe on p.15
- 1 large brown or yellow onion, sliced, then halved
- 2 Tbsp grapeseed oil
- 3 different bell peppers (yellow, orange, red or green), cut in 2" slices
- 3 cloves garlic, chopped
- ½ tsp crushed red pepper or to taste
- 1½ tsp sea salt
- 1½ 15 oz cans black beans, partially drained
- 1½ cups cooked brown rice
- ½ cup fresh or frozen corn (Trader Joe's® frozen roasted corn is perfect)

Colorful and robust, with a hint of smoky chipotle, this scrumptious dish is one you'll serve again and again!

In a large skillet on medium heat, cook the onion in the oil 3 minutes, covered when not stirring. Add peppers and stir 3 minutes or until they begin to soften. Stir in garlic, cover and cook 1 minute. Remove from heat. Add meatballs, seasonings, beans, rice and corn. Cover and cook 2 minutes, until heated through without overcooking vegetables. Or, serve the dish over a bed of rice instead of mixing it in.

Festive Pumpkin Stew

Serves 10-12 (Can be halved to serve 5-6)   Egg Free

- 1 medium-size, nicely-shaped pumpkin*
- 3 Tbsp olive oil
- 1 large yellow or brown onion, coarsely chopped, about 3 cups
- 2 cloves garlic, chopped
- 2½ lb Albacore or Ahi steaks, cubed, about 5-6 cups*
- ¾ cup chicken stock or broth
- 2 medium yams, peeled and cubed in ¾" pieces, about 4½ cups
- 3 large Yukon Gold potatoes, peeled and cubed in ¾" pieces, about 6 cups
- 2 green bell peppers, chopped in ¾" pieces, about 2½ cups
- 1¼ cups dried apricots, halved
- 1 tsp sea salt
- ½ tsp black pepper
- 3 medium tomatoes, chopped, or 1 14 oz can tomatoes, drained
- ¾ cup corn, fresh, frozen or canned, drained
- ¼ cup sherry

This is a "one of a kind" dish. Our family garnishes the pumpkin with kale and fresh, whole cranberries to form a wreath around its base on a white platter. This stew is our traditional meal on the night when our family gathers to trim the Christmas tree. Try serving it with the Burger Roll recipe baked as dinner rolls, p.57.

If using a pumpkin, wash and dry it. Carefully cut a circle around the top of the pumpkin, making a "lid" that can be replaced. Remove the pulp and seeds and set aside. You can save the seeds to be toasted in the oven. They're very nutritious.

Preheat oven to 325°. In a large skillet with a lid or a 6-qt soup pot, cook the onion in olive oil on medium-high heat about 3 minutes, then stir in the garlic and cubed fish or chicken. Cover and continue to cook 5-6 minutes, stirring often. Add the chicken stock, yams and potatoes. Stir, then cover and cook another 8 minutes. Add the green pepper, apricots, salt and pepper. Stir, cover and cook 3 minutes. Stir in the tomatoes, corn and sherry. Spoon into the prepared pumpkin, or, if not using a pumpkin, cook until just heated through and serve.

If using a pumpkin, fill it with stew and replace its top. I like to set my pumpkin in a 9" cake pan to help stabilize it. It's alright if the pumpkin is bigger than the cake pan, it will soften and form to the pan as it bakes. Place the cake pan with pumpkin in a roasting pan and put in the oven to bake 20-30 minutes, just until pumpkin begins to soften and turns a beautiful, warmer shade of orange.

*Note: This recipe can be made without the pumpkin, as a stew. It can also be halved to serve 5 to 6 instead of the party-sized meal given in the recipe above. The dish originally called for beef stew and I have reworked it using Albacore or Ahi steaks, but organic boneless, skinless chicken breasts or beef stew meat would work as well. Beef must be cooked 1-1½ hours though, in order to be tender.

Poultry & Seafood

Salmon with Creamy Pesto & Walnuts

Serves 4 Egg Free, Corn Free

- 1½ lb fresh or frozen salmon
- olive oil
- ½ cup toasted chopped walnuts
- creamy pesto sauce
- fresh basil for garnish

A dish you might enjoy at a fine restaurant. It looks wonderful, tastes heavenly, and at the same time, is high in omega 3 and omega 6.

Creamy Pesto Sauce

- 2 Tbsp olive oil
- 2½ Tbsp sorghum flour
- 1½ tsp garlic powder
- ½ cup plain rice or almond milk
- ½ cup **whole** coconut milk
- ½ tsp sea salt
- 1 cup dairy-free pesto, below

Dairy-Free Pesto

- ¾ cup coarsely chopped walnuts or pine nuts
- 2 cloves garlic
- 3 cups fresh basil leaves, lightly packed
- ⅓ tsp sea salt, or more, to taste
- 3-6 Tbsp olive oil
- 1 Tbsp lemon juice

In a blender or food processor, pulse the nuts until coarsely ground. Add the garlic and pulse a few more times. Add the basil and blend briefly. Add the salt, olive oil and lemon juice. Blend just until pesto has the consistency you desire. For a very smooth pesto, increase the olive oil.

In a 2-qt saucepan, stir together the 2 Tbsp olive oil, flour and garlic powder. Stir in 3 Tbsp of the rice or almond milk. Turn heat on to medium-low and add small amounts of milk while stirring constantly. Each time sauce begins to thicken, add a little milk until all the milk, including the coconut milk, is used. Remove from heat. Whisk in the salt and 1 cup of pesto. Cover and set aside.

Preheat grill. Reduce heat to medium-low. Spray or brush the grill generously with grapeseed oil. Brush salmon fillets with olive oil and sprinkle lightly with sea salt. Grill the salmon on a medium-low flame 4-5 minutes on each side (at approximately 325°). Salmon will flake when it is cooked. Remove salmon to a serving tray. Spoon the Creamy Pesto Sauce over the salmon and sprinkle with the walnuts. Garnish with a sprig of fresh basil.

Chicken With Rosemary & Mushroom Sauce

Serves 5-6 Egg Free, Corn Free

- 1¾ lb cauliflower (about 1 large head), stems removed, cut into chunks
- 1 14½ oz can mushroom broth or chicken stock
- 14 oz crimini mushrooms, sliced
- 2½ Tbsp fresh rosemary or 1 tsp dried
- 2 Tbsp olive oil
- 3-4 large cloves garlic, minced
- 1½ tsp sea salt, divided
- ¼ cup white wine
- 1 Tbsp grapeseed oil
- 1½-2 lb chicken or a light fish such as Mahi Mahi

In a 4-qt pot, cook the cauliflower in the chicken stock, covered 10 minutes until very soft. Remove from heat and drain, reserving ¼ cup stock. In a skillet, saute mushrooms and rosemary in the olive oil over medium heat. Cover when not stirring. Cook 6 minutes. Stir in garlic and ¼ tsp sea salt and continue cooking 2 minutes, then remove from heat. Remove the mushrooms and rosemary to a small bowl and set aside.

Into a blender, pour the drippings from the mushrooms, the cauliflower and the ¼ cup remaining chicken stock it cooked in. Blend 30 seconds. Add 1¼ tsp salt and the wine, and blend until smooth. In the same skillet used for the mushrooms, add the grapeseed oil and cook the chicken or fish over medium heat, covered, until cooked through. Mahi should be cooked on both sides and is done when it appears opaque all the way through and is moist, but flakes when separated. Return mushrooms and rosemary to the pan just long enough to heat them. Serve the chicken or Mahi covered with sauce and topped with mushrooms and rosemary.

Chicken & Kale in Garlic Wine Sauce

Serves 4-6 Egg Free, Corn Free

- 3-4 boneless, skinless chicken breasts, cut into thirds
- • garlic powder
- 1 medium red onion, sliced and halved
- 2 Tbsp olive oil, divided: 1 Tbsp + 1 Tbsp
- 3 cloves garlic, chopped
- 1½ lb kale (about one large bunch with stems), stems removed and rough chopped
- 2¼ tsp sea salt, divided: 1 tsp + 1¼ tsp
- ¾ lb cauliflower (1 very small head), or about 3 cups chopped
- 1¼ cups **light** coconut milk
- ¾ cup cooked white beans such as cannellini or navy beans, rinsed well using a strainer and drained on a paper towel
- 1½ tsp garlic powder
- ½ tsp onion powder
- 1 Tbsp dry white wine
- ¼ cup water

Preheat oven to 350°. Sprinkle the chicken lightly with sea salt and garlic powder, and place in a 9x13 baking dish. Bake uncovered 20 minutes. Check to confirm the chicken is no longer pink in center. Cover and set aside. In a skillet, saute the onion in 1 Tbsp oil 5 minutes. Cover when not stirring. Add 1 more Tbsp oil, 1 Tbsp water, chopped garlic, kale and 1 tsp salt. Stir and cook on medium heat 10 minutes or until kale is soft. Cover when not stirring. In a 3-qt pot, cook cauliflower in 3 cups water 10 minutes, covered, until very soft. Remove from heat and drain well. Into a blender, pour coconut milk and beans. Blend 30 seconds. Add cauliflower, 1¼ tsps salt, garlic powder, onion powder, wine and water. Blend 45 seconds. If sauce seems too thick, add a little water and blend again. On each plate, make a bed of kale with onions. Place a few chicken pieces on top. Ladle a generous amount of Garlic Wine Sauce over each and serve.

Coconut Ahi with Vegetables Over Rice

Serves 4-5 Egg Free, Corn Free

Sweet, spicy and exotic, this recipe is just as enticing with chicken. A wonderful dessert choice for this dinner is Coconut Tapioca Pudding on p.157.

Thai Coconut Sauce

- 1 large clove garlic, minced
- ½ Tbsp coconut oil
- 3 Tbsp green curry paste
- 1½ Tbsp coconut palm sugar
- ⅛ tsp liquid stevia
- 1½ tsp sea salt
- ¼ tsp cayenne pepper, or to taste
- 2 13½ oz cans **light** coconut milk
- 1 Tbsp tapioca flour

- 3 Tbsp coconut oil, divided: 1 Tbsp + 2 Tbsp
- 2-3 cloves garlic, minced
- 1½ lb boneless, skinless Ahi steaks, fresh or frozen and defrosted
- 1 large or 2 medium yams, about 1lb, peeled and sliced into 2 x ½" pieces
- 1 small cauliflower, about 1¼ lb, cut into bite-sized pieces
- 1 medium yellow onion, sliced into rings and then halved
- 1 lb broccoli, cut into bite-sized pieces
- ½ tsp sea salt
- 3 Tbsp coconut palm sugar
- ¼ tsp cayenne pepper
- 3 cups cooked white basmati rice
- 1¼ cups unsweetened, flaked coconut, toasted*
- ¾ cup macadamia nuts, whole or halved, toasted*

*Toasting coconut and nuts is quick and easy. For coconut, heat the oven to 350°. On a baking sheet, spread the coconut in a thin layer. Bake 5-8 minutes until golden. For macadamia nuts, on the same sheet (but not at the same time), bake 170° for 15-17 minutes.

To make sauce, use a 2-qt saucepan, cook the garlic in coconut oil over medium-low heat 2-3 minutes, just until garlic is fragrant. Remove from heat. Stir in the curry paste, coconut palm sugar, stevia, salt and cayenne pepper. Whisk in coconut milk a little at a time until smooth. Whisk in the tapioca flour until well blended. Heat the sauce over medium heat while stirring just until it begins to boil. Remove from heat and set aside.

In a skillet, melt 1 Tbsp of coconut oil and cook Ahi and garlic, covered on medium heat 4-5 minutes on each side. Remove to a plate, cover and set aside. In the same skillet, add the remaining 2 Tbsp of coconut oil. Stir fry the yams and cauliflower over medium heat 4 minutes. Cover when not stirring. Add the onion, cover and cook another 4 minutes, stirring occasionally. Last, add broccoli, cover and stir occasionally 4 minutes. Only par-cook the vegetables, not allowing them to overcook. Stop before they lose their bright colors and become too soft. Remove from heat, add the coconut palm sugar, salt and cayenne pepper. Stir just enough to mix. Make a bed of rice on each plate and spoon a portion of vegetables on top. Place a piece of Ahi over vegetables and generously spoon some Thai Coconut Sauce over each. Garnish with macadamia nuts and toasted coconut. Serve remaining sauce in a bowl or pitcher at the table.

Stir Fry over Garlic Mashed Cauli

Serves 6 — Veg & V (w/o chicken), Egg Free, Corn Free

Garlic Mashed Cauli

- 2 lb cauliflower (1 very large head), 7-8 cups chopped
- 1 Tbsp plain rice or almond milk
- ½ tsp ghee, optional
- 1¾ tsp sea salt
- 1¼-1½ tsp garlic powder
- ½ cup white beans such as cannellini or navy beans, rinsed well using a strainer and drained on a paper towel

In a 4-qt pot, cook the cauliflower in 5 cups of water, covered, about 10 minutes, until very soft. Drain well using a colander. Into a blender, put cauliflower with the milk, salt, garlic powder and ghee, if using. Blend on low speed 15 seconds. Scrape sides of blender, push cauliflower down and blend on low again. Repeat as needed. Once cauliflower is coarsely ground, add beans and blend on low speed just until smooth, but not creamed.

- 3 boneless, skinless chicken breasts, sliced in ½" by 2" strips
- 3 Tbsp olive oil, divided: 2 Tbsp + 1 Tbsp
- 4 cloves garlic, chopped, divided: 2 cloves + 2 cloves
- 1 Tbsp water
- ¾ tsp sea salt
- ¼ tsp dried oregano
- ¼ tsp dried thyme
- ¼ tsp coriander
- ⅛ tsp white pepper
- 1 medium yam, peeled, chopped into 1" pieces
- 5 cups kale, packed, (8 large leaves), sliced, stems removed
- 1 medium onion, quartered, about 2 cups
- 1 large yellow or red bell pepper, cut into chunks, about 1¾ cups
- 1 large bunch broccoli, cut into 2" pieces, about 3 cups
- 1 medium zucchini, sliced ¾" thick, then halved, about 3 cups

In a large skillet, saute the chicken in 2 Tbsp oil on medium heat 6 minutes, stirring often. Cover when not stirring. Add 2 cloves garlic and cook another 2 minutes. Chicken is done when no longer pink in center. Remove chicken to a covered bowl. In same skillet, using drippings from chicken, add 1 Tbsp olive oil, 1 Tbsp water and the salt, oregano, thyme, coriander and white pepper. Cook yams and kale covered on medium heat 7 minutes. Add onion, 2 cloves garlic, bell pepper and broccoli. Stir, cover and continue cooking 2 minutes. Add zucchini, cover and cook about 2 minutes, just until veggies are tender-crisp. Return chicken to skillet, just long enough to heat. Working quickly, on each plate spoon about ¾ cup of the Garlic Mashed Cauli. Top with a large helping of the stir-fried vegetables and chicken. Serve immediately.

We stir fry every combination of veggies as a "go-to" dinner at our house. This version is so yummy because of the creamy cauliflower, savory spices and combination of vegetables. It feels so good to finish a delicious dinner knowing that every bite was nutritious and healthy.

Chicken de Provence with Mushrooms & Caramelized Onions

Serves 6 Egg Free, Corn Free

- 1½ lb cauliflower (1 large or 2 medium heads), or 6-7 cups, cut up
- 4 cups water
- 4 Tbsp olive oil, divided, 2 Tbsp + 2 Tbsp
- 2 medium onions, divided, 1½ cups sliced + 1½ cups thinly sliced
- 3 cloves garlic
- ½ tsp Herbs de Provence
- 4-6 boneless, skinless chicken breasts
- 1 lb crimini mushrooms, sliced
- 1 tsp sea salt
- 6 sprigs of rosemary, if desired

In a 4-qt pot, cook the cauliflower in the water 10 minutes covered, until very soft. Remove from heat. In a large skillet, cook the 1½ cups sliced onion in 2 Tbsp of oil on medium heat, covered for 5 minutes. Add the garlic and cook another 2-3 minutes until onion is limp. Into a blender, pour ¾ cup of hot water from the cauliflower pot, along with ½ of the cauliflower and ½ of the onion-garlic mixture from skillet. Blend until smooth. Add remaining cauliflower and onion-garlic mixture, and blend again. Set skillet aside. Add salt and Herbs de Provence, and blend 20 seconds.

Butterfly or pound chicken breasts to ¾-1" thickness. Lightly salt and pepper each breast and the remaining onion. In the same skillet with the drippings from onion and garlic, add remaining 2 Tbsp of oil. Saute chicken with the additional 1½ cups onions and mushrooms on medium-high heat to brown chicken and caramelize the onions. Cook chicken 4 minutes on each side. Turn heat to low, cover and cook another 4-6 minutes until chicken is done. Place a piece of chicken on each plate and pour sauce generously over each. Garnish with caramelized onions and mushrooms and top with a sprig of rosemary.

This sauce is like magic. Even though this dish looks elegant, tastes rich and creamy, and seems like we have departed from dairy-free, low-fat, low-calorie eating, it is not true. In fact, all you are eating here is chicken, cauliflower, onions, mushrooms and garlic! No dairy, and in one serving there are approximately only 250 calories, 13g carbohydrates and 12g fat, while also delivering 29g protein. Wow!

Thai Coconut Chicken & Vegetables

Serves 4-5 — Egg Free, Corn Free

- 3 Tbsp green curry paste
- 2 13½ oz cans **light** coconut milk
- ½ tsp red chili pepper, to taste, optional
- ⅛ tsp liquid stevia
- 2 Tbsp coconut palm sugar
- 1½ tsp sea salt
- 2 medium boneless, skinless chicken breasts, sliced in ½" strips
- 1 Tbsp tapioca flour
- 2 Tbsp olive oil
- 1 small eggplant, chopped into ¾-1" pieces
- 1 large brown or yellow onion, sliced
- 1 lb Yukon Gold potatoes, peeled and cut into 1½ x ½" strips (about 1½ cups)
- 3 carrots, peeled and sliced
- 1¼ lb broccoli with stems removed and cut into bite-sized pieces
- 6-8 green onions, sliced in 1" lengths
- 3-4 cups cooked brown rice or white basmati rice
- ¾-1 cup raw whole cashews, toasted, on a baking sheet in a 170° oven for 15 minutes or until golden

In a 2-qt saucepan removed from heat, whisk the coconut milk into the curry paste a little at a time till blended. Whisk in the chili pepper if using, and the stevia, sugar and salt. In a bowl or plastic zip bag, mix strips of chicken with ½ cup of the coconut curry sauce. Cover and allow to marinate in the refrigerator 30-60 minutes. While chicken marinates, whisk the tapioca flour into remaining coconut curry sauce until well blended. Then, turn on heat to medium. Stir and heat until the sauce just begins to boil. Remove from heat and set aside. The sauce will continue to thicken as it cools.

In a large skillet on medium-high heat, cook chicken in marinade. Stir and cook 7-8 minutes, covering when not stirring. Remove chicken to a covered bowl and set aside. Clean the skillet, add 2 Tbsp oil and the eggplant. Stir and cook 2 minutes. Add the onion, potatoes and carrots. Cover and cook on medium-high 6 minutes, stirring occasionally. Stir in the broccoli and green onions. If necessary, add a Tbsp more oil or water. Cover and cook 2-3 minutes just until broccoli is tender-crisp. Add chicken back in with about 2 cups of coconut curry sauce. Stir and cook just until heated. Serve over rice, topped with cashews and remaining sauce.

Bon Vivant! This recipe is just as good with tilapia, sea bass, or shrimp. We love Thai food, and just like in a Thai restaurant, this dish is sweet and can be made very spicy with red chili pepper. But, by using natural sweeteners, no dairy or gluten, and the types of potatoes and rice used in all my recipes, my version is healthier and it doesn't spike blood sugar.

Tilapia with Creamy Garlic Wine Sauce

Serves 4-6 Egg Free, Corn Free

- ¾ lb cauliflower (1 very small head), or about 3 cups chopped
- 1¼ cups **light** coconut milk
- ¾ cup white beans such as cannellini or navy beans, rinsed well using a strainer and drained on a paper towel
- 1½ tsp garlic powder
- ½ tsp onion powder
- 1 Tbsp dry white wine
- ¼ cup water
- 1 Tbsp olive oil
- 4-6 pieces, or 1-1½ lb tilapia or another white fish like sea bass or snapper
- 2-3 Tbsp fresh chives, minced

How can such an elegant, delicious meal also be so nutritious and lean? It is when the main ingredients are cauliflower, beans, fish & coconut.

In a 3-qt pot, cook cauliflower in 3 cups water 10 minutes, covered, until very soft. Remove from heat and drain well. Into a blender, pour coconut milk and beans. Blend 30 seconds. Add cauliflower, 1¼ tsps sea salt, garlic powder, onion powder, wine and water. Blend 45 seconds. If sauce seems too thick, add a little water and blend again.

To pan fry: Sprinkle fish lightly with sea salt. In a large skillet, pan fry the tilapia in oil on high 2-3 minutes on each side until it begins to turn opaque. For thicker pieces of fish, cook an additional 1-2 minutes.

To bake: Preheat oven to 425°. Brush a 9x13 baking dish generously with grapeseed oil. Lightly brush the fish and sprinkle it with sea salt. Bake about 6 minutes until golden. Turn fish over and cook 2-3 minutes longer.

To serve, place a piece of fish on each plate, spoon the sauce over and sprinkle with chives.

Holiday Cranberry Chicken

Serves 4 Egg Free, Corn Free

- 4 cups fresh or frozen cranberries, rinsed and drained
- ¼ cup water
- ½ cup coconut palm sugar
- ½ tsp liquid stevia
- 3 Tbsp white wine
- 2 cloves garlic, minced
- 1 Tbsp dehydrated minced onion (dehydrated works better here than fresh)
- 4 boneless, skinless chicken breasts
- 4 cups cooked white basmati rice

In a 3-qt saucepan, cook the cranberries in ¼ cup water on medium-high heat, stirring occasionally about 10 minutes, until most of the cranberries have popped. Remove from heat. Stir in sugar, stevia and wine. Spoon half of the cranberry mixture into a small saucepan and add to it ¼ cup more water. Stir well, cover and set aside to use as sauce for chicken.

Preheat oven to 350°. Add the garlic and dehydrated onion to remaining half of cranberry mixture in the 3-qt pan. Stir to mix. Dredge each breast through cranberry mixture using a fork, coating both sides. Place chicken in an 8x11 baking dish. Spoon the cranberry-garlic-onion mixture from the 3-qt pan over top. Bake 25 minutes. Heat reserved cranberry sauce on low, stirring just until hot. Do not boil. To serve, place each chicken breast over a bed of rice on each plate and then cover with cranberry sauce from the small saucepan.

A perfect dessert to complete this ensemble is my Chocolate Decadence Pie on p.145.

Grilled Basil Shrimp & Chicken

Serves 4-6 Egg Free, Corn Free

- 1 lb uncooked large shrimp, peeled and deveined
- 2 boneless, skinless chicken breasts, cut into thirds
- 7 Tbsp olive oil, divided: ¼ cup + 3 Tbsp
- 3 Tbsp lemon juice
- 3 cloves garlic, minced, or 1 tsp garlic powder + ½ tsp garlic powder
- ¾ tsp dried basil
- ¾ tsp dried oregano
- 1½ tsp sea salt, divided: 1 tsp + ½ tsp
- 3 large or 4 medium red bell peppers, seeded, quartered and halved again into crescents

Use a large zip bag or baking dish to mix the ¼ cup olive oil, lemon juice, cloves of garlic, basil, oregano and 1 tsp salt together. Add to that the shrimp and chicken. Toss well to coat and refrigerate half hour or more to marinate. In a bowl, mix 3 Tbsp olive oil, ½ tsp garlic powder and ½ tsp salt. Add to that the bell pepper and toss until completely coated. Prepare the millet or amaranth (recipe below).

Preheat the grill. Adjust flame to medium-low. Spray or brush the grill generously with grapeseed oil. Grill the shrimp 3 minutes on each side, just until they become opaque. Grill the chicken about 5 minutes per side, just until no longer pink in center. Grill the bell pepper 4-5 minutes on each side, only until par cooked. Serve immediately over millet or amaranth.

- 1 cup millet or amaranth
- 2 cups water or chicken broth
- 1½ Tbsp olive oil
- 1 cup chopped yellow or brown onion
- 1 cup finely chopped red bell pepper
- 3 Tbsp fresh chopped basil leaves, or ¾ tsp dried
- 1 tsp sea salt

In a 2-qt saucepan, bring the water or chicken broth to a boil. Add the millet or amaranth and return to boil. Turn heat down to low and cook uncovered for 15 minutes or until the liquid is absorbed. Meanwhile, in a skillet, cook the onion in oil on medium-low heat 5 minutes. Add the bell pepper and cook, stirring occasionally, another 4 minutes. Add to that the millet or amaranth, and the basil and salt. Stir and cook just until heated through.

Your choice. Make it with shrimp and chicken, or just your favorite, but make lots, because leftovers from this dinner can also be used to prepare the Grilled Basil Shrimp & Chicken Salad, p.93. I'm not sure which dinner I like the most.

Pasta & Pizza

Lasagna

Serves 8 Veg, V & Egg Free (w/o sausage & omit eggs*), Corn Free

- 1¼ cups **whole** coconut milk, stirred well before pouring to prevent separation
- 2 14 oz cans garbanzo beans, rinsed and drained on a paper towel
- 1 tsp sea salt, divided: ½ tsp + ½ tsp
- 1 small clove garlic, or ¼ tsp garlic powder + 3 cloves garlic, minced
- 2 large eggs
- 1 tsp xanthan gum
- 1 Tbsp Italian flat leaf parsley, minced
- 11 brown rice lasagna noodles (Tinkyada® is my favorite)
- 1½ lb uncooked sweet Italian chicken sausage
- 2 Tbsp grapeseed oil + 1½ Tbsp
- 3 15 oz cans tomato sauce
- 1 6 oz can tomato paste
- ⅓ cup firmly packed fresh basil leaves, roughly chopped

Into a blender or food processor, pour the milk and ½ of garbanzo beans. Blend or process until beans are roughly ground. Add the remaining beans and blend again until creamy. Scrape sides of blender as needed. Add ½ tsp of salt, small garlic clove or garlic powder, eggs and xanthan gum. Blend for 20 seconds. Stir in parsley and set aside.

Use a wide pan (12" wide is best) to par-cook the lasagna noodles. Fill half full with water. Bring water to a boil, add 1½ Tbsp grapeseed oil and cook ½ the noodles at a time. Boil noodles gently only 6-7 minutes, or they will tear and be hard to work with. Remove noodles to a pan of cold water to stop them from continuing to cook. Drain and place noodles on wax paper to dry.

Meanwhile, pour the oil into a 6-qt pot. Squeeze the sausage meat from casings into the pot and cook on medium-high, stirring to crumble meat and cook it evenly. Continue stirring and cooking until the meat is done. Drain excess liquid. Stir in tomato sauce, tomato paste, basil, 3 cloves minced garlic and remaining ½ tsp salt. Cover and simmer 15 minutes.

Preheat oven to 350°. Into a 9x13 baking dish, spoon a small amount of sauce without sausage meat, just enough to cover the bottom. Lay 3 lasagna noodles in the pan and "patch" in the area needing noodles by cutting sections from extra noodles to fill in. Spoon ⅓ of the garbanzo mixture over the noodles. Ladle ⅓ of the sauce with sausage over that. Repeat these steps 2 more times, beginning with the noodles and ending with the sauce. Bake in oven uncovered 40-45 minutes. Remove from oven and allow to set 15 minutes before serving.

One of the things I missed most after eliminating gluten, dairy and refined sugar was lasagna. Now, I am Delighted to say that eating healthy doesn't have to mean saying good-bye to favorite dishes. Try this lasagna. I think you'll agree.

*Omit eggs & increase xanthan gum to 1¼ tsp.

Penne with Creamy Sundried Tomatoes & Sausage

Serves 4-5 Veg & V(w/o sausage), Egg Free, Corn Free

Every time we go out to Italian, I search the menu for entrees like this. Creamy and spicy, with garlic, wine, sausage and pasta...heaven! But even if I find it, I surely can't eat it because of the cream and gluten. So I order a "clean" item instead. That's why I've created this creamy, rich, GF, DF dish.

- 1½ Tbsp grapeseed oil
- 1 lb uncooked sweet Italian chicken sausage, casings removed
- ¼ cup olive oil
- ⅓ cup brown rice flour
- 1 tsp garlic powder
- 1 cup plain rice or almond milk
- 1 cup **whole** coconut milk
- 1 tsp sea salt
- 1 Tbsp red wine
- 1 cup chopped sundried tomatoes
- 10 oz brown rice penne, or other GF pasta, cooked al dente, drained well
- 3 Tbsp fresh chopped basil

In a skillet, scramble sausage in 1½ Tbsp grapeseed oil 10 minutes until cooked. Drain well, cover and set aside. In a 2-qt pan, stir together olive oil, flour, garlic powder and 3 Tbsp of the milk. Heat on medium-low. Stirring constantly, gradually add all remaining milk, as sauce thickens. Remove from heat. Stir in salt, wine and sundried tomatoes. Pour sauce into skillet with sausage. Cook on medium-low 3 minutes. Stir in cooked penne. Garnish with the basil.

Chicken & Mushroom Fettuccini with Creamy Garlic Wine Sauce

Serves 6-7 Egg Free, Corn Free

The combination of garlic, wine and mushrooms in a creamy sauce is luxurious. It sure sounds off limits, especially on pasta! Dinner guests would never dream that their fabulous meal is extremely healthy. But the good news is that this dish is totally guilt-free because it is all Delightfully Free.

- 5 Tbsp olive oil, divided
- 1½ lbs crimini mushrooms, about 8 cups, sliced
- 5 cloves garlic, minced, plus 4 cloves, pressed
- 4 medium boneless, skinless chicken breasts, cut 3" x ¾"
- ⅓ cup sorghum flour
- ½ cup plain rice or almond milk
- 1 14 oz can **light** coconut milk
- ⅓ cup white wine
- 1¾ tsp sea salt, divided: ¼ tsp plus 1½ tsp
- 12 oz brown rice fettuccini, cooked al dente, well drained
- 1½ Tbsp minced parsley or rosemary to garnish

In a large skillet, saute mushrooms in 2 Tbsp oil, covered for 5 minutes. Add minced garlic. Cook 2 minutes. Remove mushrooms to a bowl, pour remaining liquid into a cup and set aside. Add 1 Tbsp oil to skillet. Saute chicken and ¼ tsp salt 8-10 minutes, covered on medium heat, stirring occasionally, until no longer pink in center. Remove to a covered bowl. Pour drippings from skillet into the cup. Into a 2-qt pan, pour 4 Tbsp of liquid from cup. Add 2 Tbsp oil. Stir in flour, remaining 4 cloves garlic and 3 Tbsp of the milk. Heat on medium, stirring constantly. As sauce thickens, gradually add all remaining milk including coconut milk. Remove from heat. Stir in wine, 1½ tsp salt and remaining liquid. Return chicken, mushrooms and sauce to skillet. Heat and serve over fettuccini, or add fettuccini to skillet and toss. Garnish with fresh parsley or rosemary.

Creamy Garlic Sauce

Makes 3½ Cups

Veg, V, Egg Free, Corn Free

- ¾ lb cauliflower (1 very small head), 3 cups, chopped
- 1¼ cup **light** coconut milk
- ¾ cup white beans such as cannellini or navy beans, rinsed well using a strainer and drained on a paper towel
- 1¼ tsp sea salt
- 1½ tsp garlic powder
- ½ tsp onion powder
- 1 Tbsp dry white wine, optional
- ¼ cup water

In a 3-qt pot, cook cauliflower in 3 cups water, 10 minutes, covered, until very soft. Remove from heat and drain well. Into a blender, pour the coconut milk and the beans. Blend 30 seconds. Add cauliflower, salt, garlic powder, onion powder, wine, if using, and water. Blend 45 seconds. If sauce seems too thick, add a little water and blend again.

Anything tastes fabulous with this creamy sauce! Vegetables, pasta, fish...the possibilities are endless. Hard to believe it's just cauliflower, beans and coconut milk!

Old World Tomato Basil Marinara

Makes about 7 Cups   Veg, V, Egg Free, Corn Free

- 3 Tbsp olive oil
- 3-4 cloves garlic, minced
- 1 28 oz can tomato puree
- 1¾ lb fresh Roma tomatoes, chopped, or a 28 oz can crushed or diced tomatoes, drained
- 1 tsp fennel
- ¼ cup fresh basil leaves, chopped, or 1½ tsp dried
- 1 tsp dried oregano
- 3 Tbsp fresh chopped Italian flat leaf parsley
- ¼-½ tsp sea salt, or more to taste

In a 4-qt saucepan, cook the garlic in the olive oil on medium-low heat 2 minutes. Add the tomato puree and fresh or canned tomatoes. Stir in the fennel, basil, oregano, parsley and salt. Simmer uncovered 20 minutes, stirring occasionally. If using for pizza, simmer uncovered 40-50 minutes to reduce sauce.

Can be served with my Italian Meatballs over gluten-free pasta, or as the sauce on an Italian meatball sandwich using my Rosemary Rolls or another gluten-free bread. Also a great sauce for pizza, p.53.

Pasta Carbonara

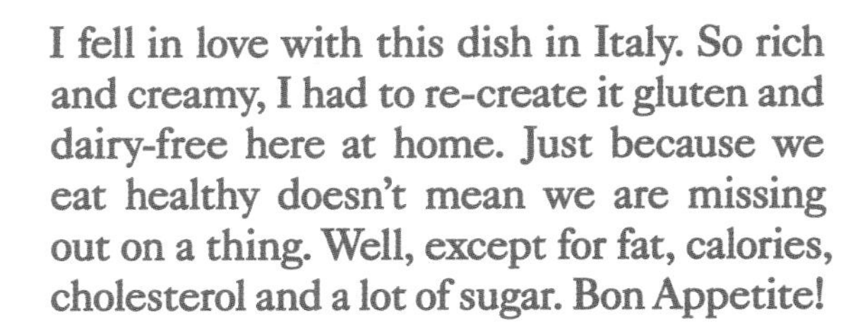

Serves 4 Veg (w/o bacon), Corn Free

- ½ lb turkey bacon
- 16 oz brown rice spaghetti, or other GF spaghetti
- 8 large fresh eggs
- ¾ cup **whole** coconut milk
- 1⅛ tsp sea salt
- ½ cup olive oil
- 8 large cloves garlic, minced
- 6 Tbsp chopped fresh Italian flat leaf parsley, divided: 3 Tbsp + 3 Tbsp
- • fresh ground pepper

I fell in love with this dish in Italy. So rich and creamy, I had to re-create it gluten and dairy-free here at home. Just because we eat healthy doesn't mean we are missing out on a thing. Well, except for fat, calories, cholesterol and a lot of sugar. Bon Appetite!

Cook the turkey bacon according to the package directions. Drain and pat dry with paper towels. Cut or crumble into small pieces and set aside. Cook spaghetti al dente and drain well. In a medium bowl, whisk the eggs. Add the milk and salt, and whisk again. Set egg mixture aside. In a 3 or 3½-qt saucepan, heat the garlic in oil. Saute on low heat 2 minutes. Remove from heat and cool 4 minutes. Place pan back on the burner and turn heat to low. As you whisk the garlic-oil, pour the egg mixture a little at a time into it. The mixture will begin to thicken. Don't let the temperature get too hot or eggs will clump. Continue to whisk and heat 2 minutes. Remove from heat. Toss with the spaghetti, cooked bacon and parsley. Serve immediately topped with fresh ground pepper and parsley.

Harvest Pasta

Serves 8 Veg & V (w/o sausage), Egg Free, Corn Free

- 6 Tbsp olive oil, divided: 3 Tbsp + 3 Tbsp
- 1 medium onion, sliced
- 2 Tbsp fresh rosemary, snipped or chopped, plus sprigs for garnish
- 3 medium carrots, peeled and sliced into thin 3" strips
- 1 large orange bell pepper, thinly sliced, about 2 cups
- 1 large yellow bell pepper, thinly sliced, about 2 cups
- 3 medium zucchini, thinly sliced long way into 3" lengths, about 3½-4 cups
- 16 oz cooked turkey Polska Kielbasa sausage, casings removed, sliced and then halved
- 1 tsp sea salt, or to taste
- 12 oz gluten-free pasta, such as brown rice spiral or fusilli

The fragrant earthiness of rosemary really makes this dish. Our family looks forward to eating this pasta in the fall. The colors and flavors remind us all of autumn.

Par-boil pasta just until al dente, drain, cover and set aside. In a large skillet, on medium-low, saute the onion and the 2 Tbsp rosemary in 3 Tbsp oil 6 minutes. Add carrots and bell peppers. Cover and continue cooking 4 minutes on medium heat, stirring occasionally. Add zucchini and cook 2-3 minutes more, just until all the vegetables are softened but their colors are still bright. Add the remaining 3 Tbsp oil, sausage and salt. Once the sausage is heated, stir in pasta. Cover and cook only until evenly heated. Serve immediately, garnished with fresh rosemary.

Creamy Pesto Fettuccini with Chicken & Artichokes

Serves 5-6 Veg & V (w/o chicken),Egg Free, Corn Free

My Italian-food loving husband says that this one is his favorite! A savory combination of flavors in a Delightfully Free pesto sauce. Most store bought pestos include dairy (usually Parmesan cheese). Make sure to use a dairy-free pesto, or you can make mine.

- 2 medium boneless, skinless chicken breasts, cut in 1½" pieces
- 2 Tbsp grapeseed oil
- ¼ cup olive oil
- ⅓ cup sorghum flour
- 1½ tsp garlic powder
- ⅔ cup plain rice or almond milk
- ⅔ cup **whole** coconut milk
- ¾ tsp sea salt
- 1⅓ cups dairy-free pesto (Recipe below)
- 1 cup pitted kalamata olives, halved
- 12 oz brown rice fettucini, cooked al dente, drained well
- 2 14 oz cans artichoke hearts in water (not marinated), drained and halved
- ½ cup toasted pine nuts

Prepare the pesto (below). Sprinkle the chicken lightly with sea salt. In a skillet, cook chicken in grapeseed oil over medium heat, stirring occasionally. Cover when not stirring. Chicken should be tender in about 8 minutes, when centers are no longer pink. Drain, cover and set aside.

In a 3-qt saucepan, stir together the olive oil, flour and garlic powder. Add 3 Tbsp of the milk. Turn heat to medium-low. Stirring constantly, add small amounts of the milk at a time. As soon as the sauce begins to bubble and thicken, add more milk until all the milk has been used, including the coconut milk. Remove from heat. Whisk in the salt and pesto. Pour pesto sauce and olives into the skillet with chicken. Stir over medium heat until the sauce just begins to bubble. Stir in the pasta, cover and heat 2 minutes. Add the artichoke hearts. Stir just enough to heat, but not enough to break up artichoke hearts or make the pasta mushy. Serve with toasted pine nuts sprinkled over each serving.

Dairy-Free Pesto

- 1 cup coarsely-chopped walnuts or pine nuts
- 3 cloves garlic
- 4 cups fresh basil leaves, lightly packed
- ½ tsp sea salt, or more, to taste
- ¼ cup olive oil, or more for smoother texture
- 1½ Tbsp lemon juice

In a blender or food processor, pulse the nuts until they are coarsely ground. Add the garlic and pulse a couple more times. Add the remaining ingredients and blend until the pesto has the consistency you desire. For a very smooth pesto, increase the olive oil.

YUMMY

Mac & "Cheese"

Makes 3 Entrees or 6 Side Dishes Veg, V, Egg Free, Corn Free

- 3 Tbsp olive oil
- ¼ cup sorghum flour
- 1 tsp garlic powder
- 1 cup plain rice milk or almond milk
- ½ cup **whole** coconut milk
- 1 tsp sea salt
- 2 dashes nutmeg
- 2 cups uncooked brown rice elbow macaroni or corkscrew or your favorite GF pasta
- 2 golden beets, optional*
- • GF, minimally processed chicken or turkey hot dogs, such as Trader Joe's® brand, sliced, optional

*Note: To enhance the color of the Mac & "Cheese" to a deeper golden yellow, use 2 golden beets, washed and quartered, and ¾ cup water, or a pinch of turmeric. A small percentage of people have sensitivities to beets. If you are among that group, simply eliminate the beet juice from this recipe and use the turmeric.

If using beets for enhanced color:

In a small saucepan, bring beets and ¾ cup water to a boil. Reduce heat and simmer covered 1 hour, checking often to ensure that the water doesn't evaporate completely. You will end up with 1-2 Tbsp deep, yellow-colored water. If more than 2 Tbsp remains, remove the lid and continue to cook on low. Remove from heat when there is only about 2 Tbsp of water remaining. Remove the beets and save them to use as a side dish or sliced in salads.

Cook pasta just until al dente, and drain. Meanwhile, to make the sauce, in a 3-qt saucepan, stir together the olive oil, flour, garlic powder, and 3 Tbsp of the milk. Turn heat on to medium-low and stirring constantly, continue to add small amounts of milk to the pan. Each time the sauce begins to thicken, add a little milk, including the coconut milk until all the milk is stirred in. Remove from heat. If using beet juice, stir it in. Add the salt, nutmeg and, if desired, a pinch of turmeric for color. Stir in the drained pasta and mix to coat. Optional: Add sliced chicken or turkey hot dogs.

This recipe is one of my personal favorites because it puts Mac & "Cheese" back on the plate for those children (even grown up ones) who are gluten, casein or lactose intolerant. What's really great about enhancing the golden color of your Mac & "Cheese" using beets is that, along with the color, which kids will love, you are sneaking in nutritional goodness. In addition to providing important vitamins and minerals, beets also have antioxidant properties that help boost cardiovascular health, fight inflammation, and prevent colon cancer.

Pizza Crust

Makes One 16" Crust

Veg, V, Egg Free, Corn Free, **Yeast Free**

- 1 cup garbanzo bean flour
- ¾ cup tapioca flour
- ½ cup arrowroot flour
- ¼ cup brown rice flour
- 1 tsp aluminum-free, GF baking powder
- 1 tsp baking soda
- 1¼ tsp sea salt
- ½ tsp dried basil leaves
- ¾ tsp garlic powder
- 1 tsp xanthan gum
- ¾ cup + 2 Tbsp warm water
- 3 Tbsp olive oil
- 2 16" lengths of wax or parchment paper, or better, one 16" length, wide enough to cover pizza pan

Preheat oven to 400°. Spray a 16" pizza pan with grapeseed oil. Also generously spray 1 side of the 2 sheets or the 1 larger sheet of wax or parchment paper, and set aside. In a large bowl, using a whisk, slowly stir all dry ingredients. These flours are very light and can puff right out of the bowl. Add olive oil and water. Mix well. Form a ball in the middle of the pan. Cover dough with prepared parchment or wax paper to keep it from sticking to the rolling pin, and using the rolling pin, spread it out to the edges of the pan, then carefully remove paper. Bake on bottom rack of oven 12 minutes until center is firm to the touch. Add your choice of sauce and toppings. Continue baking approximately 12 minutes, until edges are golden, or longer for a crispier crust.

Sausage & Pepper Pizza

Makes One 16" Pizza

Veg & V (w/o sausage), Egg Free, Corn Free, **Yeast Free**

Red Sauce

- 1 Tbsp olive oil
- 1 clove garlic, minced
- 1 8 oz can tomato puree
- 10 oz fresh Roma tomatoes, chopped and drained, or one 8 oz can crushed or diced tomatoes, drained well
- ⅓ tsp fennel
- 1½ Tbsp fresh basil leaves, chopped, or ½ tsp dried
- ¾ tsp fresh oregano, or ⅓ tsp dried (I prefer dried)
- 1 Tbsp fresh chopped Italian flat leaf parsley
- ⅛ tsp sea salt, or to taste

Toppings

- 8-10 oz any variety of fully cooked chicken sausage, sliced
- 4 medium mushrooms, about ⅔ cup, thinly sliced
- 1 medium green bell pepper, thinly sliced
- ½ small onion, thinly sliced or chopped, about ¾ cup
- 3 Tbsp olive oil

In a 2-qt saucepan, cook garlic in oil on medium-low heat 2 minutes. Drain canned tomatoes or fresh tomatoes well. Add tomato puree and fresh or canned tomatoes. Stir in fennel, basil, oregano, parsley and salt. Simmer uncovered 20-30 minutes to reduce and thicken sauce. Preheat oven to 400°. After baking pizza crust (recipe above) the initial 12 minutes, spread Red Sauce up to ¾ inch from edge. Toss mushrooms, pepper and onion in 3 Tbsp oil. Scatter all toppings over pizza. Bake 10-12 minutes on lower oven rack or until toppings are softened and crust edge is golden.

Veggie Pizza with Creamy Garlic Sauce

Makes One 16" Pizza   Veg, V, Egg Free, Corn Free, **Yeast Free**

Creamy Garlic Sauce

- ¼ cup olive oil
- ⅓ cup sorghum flour
- 3¼ tsp garlic powder
- ½ cup plain rice or almond milk
- ¾ cup **whole** coconut milk
- 1¾ tsp sea salt
- 1/16 tsp nutmeg

Toppings

- 1 large tomato, sliced thin
- 6 oz canned or frozen **unmarinated** artichoke hearts, drained and halved
- ⅓ cup black olives, sliced
- 1 small zucchini, sliced thin, about ¾ cup
- 1 medium yellow or orange bell pepper, sliced thin
- 4 medium mushrooms, sliced thin, about ⅔ cup
- ½ small yellow or red onion, sliced thin, about ¾ cup
- 4 green onions, sliced, about ¾ cup
- ½ cup fresh whole basil leaves
- 2½ Tbsp olive oil

In a 2-qt saucepan, stir the oil, flour and garlic powder together. Stir in 3 Tbsp of the milk until well blended. Turn heat on to medium-low, and stirring constantly, continue to add small amounts of milk, including coconut milk, to the pan. Each time the sauce begins to thicken, add a little milk until all the milk is stirred in. Turn off heat and remove pan. Stir in salt and nutmeg and set aside. In a large bowl, toss artichokes, zucchini, bell peppers, mushrooms, both onions and basil in 2½ Tbsp olive oil and ½ tsp sea salt. Preheat oven to 400°. After baking the pizza crust (p.53) the initial 12 minutes, spread the Creamy Garlic Sauce up to ¾ inch from the edge. Scatter all toppings over the sauce. Sprinkle pizza with sea salt. Bake on bottom rack of oven 10-12 minutes or until toppings are softened and edges of crust are golden.

Creamy Pesto Pizza

Makes One 16" Pizza   Veg & V (w/o sausage), Egg Free, Corn Free, **Yeast Free**

Dairy-Free Pesto

- ¾ cup chopped walnuts or pine nuts
- 2 cloves garlic
- 3 cups fresh basil leaves, lightly packed
- ⅓ tsp sea salt, or more, to taste
- 3-6 Tbsp olive oil
- 1 Tbsp lemon juice

Creamy Pesto Sauce

- 2 Tbsp olive oil
- 3 Tbsp sorghum flour
- 1½ tsp garlic powder
- ½ cup plain rice or almond milk
- ½ cup **whole** coconut milk
- ¾ tsp sea salt
- 1 cup dairy-free pesto

Toppings

- 8-10 oz cooked Italian-style chicken sausage, sliced, or cooked by scrambling in a pan
- ½ small red onion, thinly sliced and tossed in 1 Tbsp olive oil
- 1 cup chopped sundried tomatoes

For pesto, pulse nuts in blender or food processor until coarsely ground. Add garlic and pulse again. Add basil and blend briefly. Add salt, olive oil and lemon juice. Blend just until pesto has the desired consistency. For very smooth pesto, increase olive oil. To make sauce, in a 2-qt saucepan, stir together oil, flour, garlic powder and 3 Tbsp of the milk. Turn heat on to medium-low. Stirring constantly, add a little milk. Each time sauce begins to thicken, add a little more until all, including coconut milk, is used. Remove from heat. Whisk in salt and 1 cup pesto. Cover and set aside. Preheat oven to 400°. After baking pizza crust (p.53) the initial 12 minutes, spread Creamy Pesto Sauce up to ¾ inch from edge. Sprinkle sausage and onion evenly on top. Bake 6 minutes on lower oven rack. Remove from oven and spread sundried tomatoes over top. Bake another 6 minutes or until onion is softened and edges of crust are golden.

Breads & Muffins

Cornbread

Serves 8 — Veg, V & Egg Free (w/ egg replacer)

- 1 cup cornmeal, fine grind
- ⅓ cup + 1 Tbsp brown rice flour
- 1 Tbsp coconut flour
- ¼ tsp xanthan gum
- ½ tsp baking soda
- 1 Tbsp + 1 tsp aluminum-free, GF baking powder
- ¾ tsp sea salt
- 3 Tbsp coconut oil
- 3 Tbsp coconut nectar
- ⅛ tsp liquid stevia
- 1 large egg, whisked
- ¾ cup + 2 Tbsp vanilla rice or almond milk

You would never know it's GF! This cornbread is a wonderful complement to most of my soups or any of the BBQ salad recipes. It pairs perfectly with Lentil Stew.

Preheat oven to 375°. Brush or spray an 8x8 pan or a muffin tin with grapeseed oil. In a medium bowl, stir together the dry ingredients using a wire whisk. Add the coconut oil, coconut nectar, stevia, egg and milk. Stir until well combined. **Rest the batter for 10 minutes.** Turn into the pan or tin, and bake for 18 minutes, or until the center is firm and slightly "springy" to the touch.

Burger Rolls (PHOTO P.18)

Makes 5 Rolls — Veg, Corn Free, **Yeast Free**

- ⅔ cup sorghum flour
- ⅔ cup tapioca flour
- ⅓ cup arrowroot flour
- ⅓ cup coconut flour
- 1 tsp baking soda
- 1 Tbsp + 1 tsp aluminum-free, GF baking powder
- ½ tsp xanthan gum
- ⅔ cup egg whites
- 1 Tbsp grapeseed oil, plus extra
- 2½ Tbsp coconut palm sugar
- 1 tsp sea salt
- 1¼ cup water
- 4 tsp dehydrated minced onion, optional
- 1 tsp chia, poppy or sesame seeds, optional
- • organic all vegetable shortening, such as Spectrum®

I chose not to use yeast because some people cannot tolerate it. It was especially tricky to make a GF and yeast-free roll that still seems light and fluffy. After many tries, I developed this roll which is tasty and works well with a burger. This roll recipe can also be baked in a muffin tin and served as dinner rolls.

Preheat oven to 350°. Use five 2-cup size, round oven-safe bowls or ramekins, 4½-5" in diameter. (Anchor® and Pyrex® make these.) Grease bowls generously with shortening and dust with sorghum flour. Sift each flour into a medium bowl. Discard any coarse granules. Add baking soda, baking powder and xanthan gum, and sift again. In another bowl, whisk egg whites. Whisk in oil, sugar, salt and water. With whisk, stir wet ingredients into dry ingredients until smooth. Dough will be thin, like batter. Divide dough between the baking dishes and jiggle to spread dough evenly. Gently brush the tops generously with grapeseed oil. Sprinkle with onion and/or seeds, if desired. Bake 25 minutes, or until toothpick comes out clean. Tops will be golden and slightly springy to the touch. Cool on a rack 8 minutes. Run a knife around edge of each and turn rolls out onto the rack to cool 8 minutes more. With a serrated knife, slice the rolls open and enjoy the burger of your choice.

Seeded Quick Bread

Makes One Loaf   Veg, V & Egg Free (w/ egg replacer), Corn Free, **Yeast Free**

- ½ cup arrowroot flour
- ¼ cup brown rice flour
- 1 cup tapioca flour
- ⅓ cup sorghum flour
- 1 tsp baking soda
- 2 tsp aluminum-free, GF baking powder
- 1 tsp sea salt
- ½ tsp ground cardamom
- 1 tsp xanthan gum
- 2 large eggs
- ¼ cup grapeseed oil
- 3 Tbsp coconut palm sugar
- 1 cup water

Seed Mix

- ¼ cup shelled and lightly toasted pumpkin seeds
- 1 Tbsp chia seeds
- 1 Tbsp toasted sesame seeds

Tired of dry dense GF bread? Try mine!

You probably think I included this recipe because we GF people want to eat bread every chance we get, right? That's true, but I also have a nutrition agenda. This bread has lots of nutrients, especially in all those seeds. One Tbsp of chia seeds alone has 2,282mg omega 3, 752mg omega 6, 5g fiber, 3g protein and no sugar. The pumpkin and sesame seeds are similar in their nutritional content.

Toast the pumpkin and sesame seeds, if not already toasted, in a 325° oven on a baking sheet 4 minutes. Stir all seeds together in a small bowl. Preheat oven to 350°. Brush or spray a loaf pan with grapeseed oil. In a large bowl, carefully stir the 4 flours, baking soda, baking powder, salt, cardamom and xanthan gum together using a wire whisk. Move slowly because the flours are very light and can puff right out of the bowl. Lift and separate the flour mixture by allowing it to pour through the whisk. In another bowl, whisk the eggs. Add the oil, sugar and water, and whisk until the sugar is dissolved. Stir the wet ingredients into the dry ingredients. Use the whisk to blend. Pour in all but 2 Tbsp of the seed mixture and stir just enough to mix. **Rest the batter for 10 minutes.** Spoon into the loaf pan and spread it to the edges. Tap the pan on the counter a couple of times to release any air bubbles. Sprinkle the remaining seeds over the top and gently pat down with fingers. Bake 15 minutes, and rotate pan 180 degrees. Continue baking 20 minutes more (totalling 35 minutes), or until a toothpick inserted in the center comes out clean. Cool on a rack 15 minutes. Carefully turn out of the pan, slice and enjoy!

Moist, light and tender, this bread is delicious and versatile. Use it for sandwiches or toast it for breakfast. Vary the taste by adding other ingredients. For example, substitute just one kind of seed in place of the combination. Mix 1-2 Tbsp in the dough, plus 2 Tbsp for the top. Add 1½-2 tsp dried dill weed and 1½ Tbsp dehydrated, minced onion to the dough, yum! – or – use only the pumpkin seeds, chopped, and stir into the dough 1-2 tsp fresh thyme or rosemary or basil/oregano. Mince fresh onion very finely and add 2 Tbsp. For a sweeter bread, replace the seeds with walnuts or pecans. Increase the coconut palm sugar to ½ cup. Add 1½ tsp cinnamon and ⅓ cup raisins or unsweetened cranberries or cherries. Have fun!

Rosemary Rolls

Makes 10 Rolls

Veg, V, Egg Free, Corn Free, **Yeast Free**

- 3 Tbsp olive oil, plus extra
- 2 tsp + 1½ tsp fresh rosemary leaves, chopped
- ½ cup garbanzo bean flour
- 1 cup tapioca flour
- ½ cup arrowroot flour
- ¼ cup sorghum flour
- 3 Tbsp brown rice flour
- 2 tsp aluminum-free, GF baking powder
- 1 tsp baking soda
- 1 tsp sea salt
- ½ tsp dried basil
- ¾ tsp garlic powder
- ¾ tsp xanthan gum
- 1 cup warm water
- • sea salt crystals in a grinder

Crusty on the outside, soft on the inside, this hearty Italian-style roll is so flavorful you'll want to bake a second batch. The combination of rosemary and sea salt with crunch is addictive! If you've gone a while without bread, hurry and make some. I hope you'll be as excited about them as I am.

In a small skillet, saute the 2 tsp rosemary in the 3 Tbsp oil on low 2 minutes. Remove from heat and set aside. Preheat oven to 400°. Brush or spray a baking sheet or muffin tin with grapeseed oil. In a medium bowl, whisk all 11 dry ingredients together. Stir in the water and the olive oil with rosemary from the skillet. Combine well. Dough will be soft and sticky. **Rest the dough 10 minutes.** To bake, either fill a muffin tin only ½ full with dough, or, for a more traditional looking roll, rub hands with a little olive oil and with hands, roll 2¼" balls of dough. Place on baking sheet 1" apart. Brush each roll with olive oil and sprinkle with fresh ground sea salt crystals and the remaining rosemary. Bake 20-22 minutes. Rolls are ready when they have risen, formed cracks, and are turning golden. Refrigerate or freeze any leftover rolls. They freeze and reheat very nicely.

Harvest Pumpkin Bread

Makes One Loaf — Veg, V & Egg Free (w/ egg replacer), Corn Free

- 3 large eggs
- 1⅓ cups canned pumpkin
- ¼ cup grapeseed oil
- 2 tsp vanilla
- ¾ cup coconut palm sugar
- ¾ tsp liquid stevia
- ½ cup brown rice flour
- ⅓ cup coconut flour
- ⅔ cup arrowroot flour
- 1½ tsp baking soda
- 1½ tsp aluminum-free, GF baking powder
- ¾ tsp sea salt
- ½ tsp xanthan gum
- 1¼ tsp cinnamon
- 1 tsp ground cloves
- ½ tsp ginger
- ½ cup chopped walnuts or pecans, optional
- ⅓ cup golden or dark raisins, optional
- ¼ cup chopped pumpkin seeds, optional

Warm your home and family with Harvest Pumpkin Bread when it's cold outside. Double for 2 loaves. A second loaf can be given away or frozen for later.

Preheat oven to 340°. Brush or spray a loaf pan with grapeseed oil. In a large bowl, whisk the eggs. Whisk in the pumpkin, oil, vanilla, sugar & stevia. Stir in the 3 flours, baking powder, baking soda, salt, xanthan gum, cinnamon, cloves & ginger. Add nuts, seeds and/or raisins, if using. Spoon into pan and spread evenly to the edges. Bake about 35-40 minutes. A toothpick will come out slightly sticky. Cool in pan on a rack 20 minutes before turning out.

Banana Chocolate Chip Bread

Makes One Loaf — Veg, V & Egg Free (w/ egg replacer), Corn Free

- 4 large eggs
- ¾ cup coconut palm sugar
- 3 Tbsp grapeseed oil
- 2 ripe, medium bananas, about ¾ cup, mashed
- 1 tsp cinnamon
- ¾ tsp sea salt
- 1½ tsp baking soda
- 1½ tsp aluminum-free, GF baking powder
- ¼ cup brown rice flour
- ½ cup coconut flour
- ¼ tsp xanthan gum
- ⅓ cup finely chopped, DF dark chocolate,* optional
- ⅔ cup chopped walnuts, optional

Wonderful warm or at room temperature. A favorite at gatherings. Double the recipe for 2 loaves. Freeze the second loaf for when unexpected guests arrive.

Preheat oven to 340°. Brush or spray a 9 inch loaf pan with grapeseed oil. In a mixing bowl, whisk the eggs. Add the coconut sugar and whisk again. Add the oil, bananas, cinnamon, salt, baking soda and baking powder, and whisk again until all ingredients are blended. Stir in the 2 flours and then the xanthan gum. If using nuts and/or chocolate, stir them in, reserving a couple of tablespoons of each to sprinkle on top, if desired. If putting chocolate chips on top, wait until later to add them per instructions below.

Bake about 35 minutes or until a toothpick inserted in center comes out clean. Note: If using chocolate chips, remove loaf from oven after 25 minutes to sprinkle them on top. Quickly return loaf to oven to finish baking. Cool on a rack at least 20 minutes. Run a knife around edges of loaf and turn it out of the pan to finish cooling on rack. Be careful not to touch the chocolate chips on top, if using them, because they won't be hardened yet.

*See note on chocolate chips on p.7

Latte Muffins

Makes about 17 Muffins

Veg, V & Egg Free (w/ egg replacer), Corn Free

- 4 large eggs
- ⅓ cup grapeseed oil
- 1¾ tsp liquid stevia
- 1½ cups canned pumpkin
- ½ cup warm water
- ⅓ cup instant decaf coffee crystals
- 3 cups GF oat bran
- 1 Tbsp arrowroot flour
- 1 Tbsp water
- 1½ tsp sea salt
- 2½ tsp baking soda
- 1½ Tbsp aluminum-free, GF baking powder
- ½ tsp xanthan gum
- 1½ cups coconut palm sugar
- ½ cup chopped pitted dates
- 1 cup chopped walnuts, optional
- 1 tsp toasted flaxseed, optional

What could be better than a Latte Muffin fresh out of the oven with a cup of hot coffee? A slice of quiche to go with it, of course!

In a large bowl, whisk the eggs. Whisk in the oil, stevia and pumpkin. Stir the instant coffee into the ½ cup warm water until dissolved, and add that to the egg mixture. Stir in the bran, flour, 1 Tbsp water, salt, baking soda, baking powder and xanthan gum. Add the sugar and stir well. Add the dates and walnuts, if desired. **Rest the batter for 10 minutes before filling tins.** Letting the batter rest before filling the tins makes the difference between flat, textureless muffins and crested, picture-perfect ones. Preheat oven to 350°. Brush or spray tins with grapeseed oil or line with paper baking cups. Fill tins almost full, sprinkle a pinch of the flaxseeds on top of each muffin, if desired, and bake about 17 minutes or until center of muffins feel firm to the touch. Cool tins on a wire rack for 5 minutes, then remove muffins from tins using a knife, if not using paper liners. Allow to cool completely on a wire rack or serve warm. Store in an airtight container in refrigerator.

I believe that breakfast should be high in protein and fiber, and low in refined sugar.

These are wholesome muffins and pancakes made for the most part without flour. Oat bran and eggs are the 2 predominant ingredients. Coconut palm sugar and coconut nectar are natural sugars, but they are organic and unrefined which gives them a low glycemic index so that they do not spike blood sugar the way conventional, refined sugars do. On top of that, fiber, which is what oat bran is essentially, helps control the problem of high blood sugar. Fiber is considered to be an ally in managing high blood sugar because it doesn't require insulin to be digested. For this reason, I use oat bran in almost all of my muffins and pancakes.

Oat Pancakes

Makes about 12 Pancakes — Veg, V & Egg Free (w/ egg replacer), Corn Free

- 3 large eggs
- ¼ cup coconut palm sugar
- 1¼ cups GF oat bran
- ¼ cup + 1 Tbsp grapeseed oil
- 3 Tbsp rice or almond milk
- 15-20 drops liquid stevia
- 1 tsp aluminum-free, GF baking powder
- ¼ tsp sea salt
- 1½ tsp cinnamon
- ⅛ tsp nutmeg
- ½ cup chopped walnuts, optional

This is the basic recipe for Oat Pancakes. We love them with sliced bananas and a little coconut nectar. Here are some other fun variations. In the fall, we add to the cinnamon, 1½ tsp pumpkin spices or ½ tsp cloves. The nuts can be substituted with raisins, or, on a special day, chocolate chips. In the summer, sliced strawberries, blueberries and peaches with a dollop of Whipped Topping, p.159, make them the centerpiece of a seasonal breakfast. I like that they can be served again another day by reheating them in the toaster.

Spray a griddle with grapeseed oil and heat it up. In a bowl, whisk eggs with sugar. Stir in bran and remaining ingredients. Reduce heat to low or medium-low. Spoon batter onto griddle in pancake-sized rounds. Help spread the batter so the pancakes are not too thick. The trick is to keep the heat low so that they cook slowly on the inside before getting too done on the outside. When bubbles appear, they are ready to be flipped carefully with a spatula. They are done when golden brown.

Cinnamon Pecan Coffee Cake

Serves 6-8 — Veg, V & Egg Free (w/ egg replacer), Corn Free

- ¼ cup organic all vegetable shortening, such as Spectrum®
- ¾ cup coconut palm sugar
- 2 large eggs
- ½ tsp vanilla
- ½ cup garbanzo bean flour
- ⅓ cup potato starch
- 1½ Tbsp corn starch
- ½ tsp aluminum-free, GF baking powder
- ½ tsp baking soda
- ½ tsp xanthan gum
- ¼ tsp sea salt
- 3 Tbsp vanilla rice or almond milk
- 1¼ cups chopped pecans

Cinnamon Sauce

- ¾ cup water
- ¼ cup coconut palm sugar
- ¼ tsp liquid stevia
- ⅛ tsp, plus a pinch, sea salt
- 1½ tsp cinnamon
- 1½ tsp tapioca flour
- 1 tsp ghee, optional for a buttery flavor

In a 1-qt saucepan, stir water, sugar, stevia, salt and cinnamon together. Whisk in the tapioca flour and ghee, if using. Turn heat on to medium-low and stir until sauce reaches a low boil. Continue to stir and cook 1 minute. Remove from heat and set aside. Sauce will continue to thicken as it cools. Preheat oven to 350°. Spray an 8x8 pan with grapeseed oil. In a bowl, cream shortening and sugar using a mixer. Add eggs and beat again. Mix in remaining ingredients, except for pecans and cinnamon sauce. Pour into pan and sprinkle with pecans. Bake 20-25 minutes, just until firm in center and a toothpick comes out clean. Cool on a rack 15 minutes. Pour cinnamon sauce over top and serve. Or, turn out onto a platter, pour sauce over top and serve.

Lemon Strawberry Muffins

Makes about 14 Muffins — Veg, V & Egg Free (w/ egg replacer), Corn Free

- 4 large eggs
- ½ cup grapeseed oil
- ⅓ cup coconut nectar
- ⅔ cup coconut palm sugar
- 1 tsp liquid stevia
- 1½ Tbsp water
- ½ tsp vanilla
- 2 tsp baking soda
- 1 Tbsp aluminum-free, GF baking powder
- 1 tsp sea salt
- 2 cups GF oat bran
- ¼ cup arrowroot flour
- 2½ Tbsp coconut flour
- ½ tsp xanthan gum
- 2 Tbsp lemon juice
- ½ cup grated lemon zest
- 1⅔ cups strawberries, about 8 medium strawberries, chopped

These muffins are perfect for a spring or summer brunch, luncheon or tea. They look so pretty on the platter and taste just like the essence of summer.

Preheat oven to 325°. Spray muffin tins with grapeseed oil or use paper liners. In a bowl, whisk the eggs. Whisk in oil, coconut nectar, sugar, stevia, water and vanilla. Add baking soda, baking powder and salt, whisking until smooth. Stir in dry ingredients, ending with xanthan gum, and mix well. Fold in lemon juice, zest, and strawberries. **Rest batter 10 minutes.** Fill tins almost full and bake 20 minutes, or until center of muffins feel firm to the touch. Cool on rack 5 minutes. Remove using a knife to loosen around muffins, if not using paper liners. Cool completely or serve warm.

Banana Nut Muffins

Makes about 16 Muffins — Veg, V & Egg Free (w/ egg replacer), Corn Free

- 4 large eggs
- ⅓ cup + 2 Tbsp grapeseed oil
- 1 Tbsp water
- 1 cup + 1 Tbsp cocunut palm sugar
- 1¼ tsp liquid stevia
- 3 large, ripe bananas, mashed
- 3 cups GF oat bran
- 1 Tbsp arrowroot flour
- 1⅓ tsp sea salt
- ½ tsp xanthan gum
- 2 tsp baking soda
- 2½ tsp aluminum-free, GF baking powder
- 1¾ tsp cinnamon
- ¼ tsp ground cloves
- 1½ cups chopped walnuts, optional

Sweet and delicious. Because we can do magic with natural sweeteners, each has only about 13.5g sugar. Compare that to most muffins that average 3-4 times more without the added benefits of being GF, DF and free of refined sugars.

Preheat oven to 340°. In a large bowl, whisk the eggs. Whisk in oil, water, sugar and stevia. Stir in bananas. In another bowl, whisk bran, flour, salt, xanthan gum, baking soda, baking powder, cinnamon, and cloves. Stir dry mixture into egg mixture. Stir in walnuts. **Rest batter 10 minutes.** Spray tins with grapeseed oil or use paper liners. Fill tins ¾ full and bake about 16 minutes or until a toothpick comes out clean. Cool on a rack 5 minutes. Remove using a knife to loosen around muffins if not using paper liners. Cool completely or serve warm.

Blueberry Banana Muffins

Makes about 14 Muffins — Veg, V & Egg Free (w/ egg replacer), Corn Free

- 3 large eggs
- ¼ cup grapeseed oil
- ¾ cup coconut palm sugar
- ½ tsp liquid stevia
- 3 large, ripe bananas, mashed
- 1 tsp sea salt
- 1½ tsp baking soda
- 1½ tsp aluminum-free, GF baking powder
- ½ tsp xanthan gum
- 1 tsp cinnamon
- ½ cup sorghum flour
- ⅔ cup tapioca flour
- ¼ cup coconut flour
- ⅓ cup arrowroot flour
- ⅔ cup fresh or frozen blueberries

Preheat oven to 350°. Brush muffin tins generously with grapeseed oil or use paper baking cups. In a large bowl, whisk the eggs. Whisk in the oil, sugar, stevia, mashed bananas, salt, baking soda, baking powder, xanthan gum and cinnamon. Slowly whisk in all four flours until blended (They are lightweight and easily displaced). Stir in the blueberries without over-mixing. **Rest the batter 10 minutes before filling tins.** Allowing the batter to rest before filling the tins makes the difference between flat, textureless muffins and crested, picture-perfect ones. Fill the tins only ⅔ full and bake about 14 minutes or until a toothpick comes out clean. Cool tins on a rack 5 minutes, then remove using a knife to loosen around each muffin, if not using paper liners.

Miss those light, caky muffins? Try these.

Pumpkin Spice Muffins

Makes 18-20 Muffins — Veg, V & Egg Free (w/ egg replacer), Corn Free

- 6 large eggs
- ⅓ cup grapeseed oil
- 1 Tbsp water
- 3 cups GF oat bran
- 1 15 oz can pumpkin
- 2 tsp vanilla
- 1 cup + 2 Tbsp coconut palm sugar
- 1½ tsp liquid stevia
- 1 Tbsp arrowroot flour
- 1½ Tbsp aluminum-free, GF baking powder
- 2½ tsp baking soda
- 1½ tsp sea salt
- 1½ Tbsp cinnamon
- 1½ Tbsp pumpkin spice blend
- ½ tsp cloves
- ¼ tsp xanthan gum
- ¾ cup golden or dark raisins
- 1 cup chopped walnuts, optional

Preheat oven to 350°. Brush or spray muffin tins with grapeseed oil. In a large bowl, whisk eggs with oil and water. Stir in the bran, pumpkin and remaining ingredients. **Rest the batter for 10 minutes before filling muffin tins.** Spoon batter into tins making them almost full. Bake 15-16 minutes. Muffins are ready when tops feel firm to the touch. Let muffins cool in tins on a rack 3-4 minutes, then loosen around the edges with a knife. Remove muffins from the tins to a wire rack to cool completely or serve warm.

Even the thought of these muffins makes me feel like it is autumn. They are perfect on a cold or rainy morning with a hot cup of tea or coffee, and one of my egg dishes. I hope your family will love them as much as mine does.

Eggs, Fruit & Cereal

Broccoli Zucchini Quiche

Serves 8 Veg, Corn Free

- 2 Tbsp grapeseed oil
- ½ cup celery, finely chopped
- 1 cup red onion, chopped
- ¾ cup sliced mushrooms
- 1½ cups broccoli, chopped in ½" pieces
- 1½ cups zucchini, chopped in ½" pieces
- 2 cloves garlic, minced
- 3 Tbsp fresh sage, minced
- 8 large eggs
- 1 cup + 2 Tbsp **light** coconut milk
- 1¾ tsp sea salt
- 5 dashes nutmeg
- 1 cup cooked brown rice

Picture perfect and savory, a big hit for brunch. Easily halved and made in one 9" pie dish, or doubled for two 9x13 dishes.

Preheat oven to 350°. Spray a 9x13 baking dish, two 9" pie dishes, or individual tins with grapeseed oil. In a skillet, cook celery, onion and mushrooms in oil on medium-low heat 4 minutes, stirring occasionally. Cover when not stirring. Add broccoli and cook 2 minutes. Add zucchini, garlic and sage, cover when not stirring and cook 4 minutes. Remove from heat. Drain liquid. In a bowl, whisk eggs. Add coconut milk, salt and nutmeg, and whisk again. Add rice and vegetables to egg mixture. Mix well and pour into dish. Bake a 9x13 dish 35 minutes, smaller tins 14 minutes, or 9" dishes 18-20 minutes. Test to be sure; quiche is ready when a knife inserted in center comes out clean and it feels firm when lightly touched.

Spinach Mushroom Quiche

Serves 8 Veg, Corn Free

- 5 brown rice tortillas
- • olive oil
- 6 eggs
- ½ cup soy-free mayonnaise such as Soy-Free Vegenaise®
- ¾ cup **light** coconut milk
- 1¼ tsp sea salt
- ¼ tsp white pepper
- ¼ tsp coriander
- ¼ tsp nutmeg
- 2 cups finely chopped red onion
- 2 Tbsp grapeseed oil
- 3 cups sliced brown mushrooms (10oz)
- 6-7 cups lightly packed fresh spinach (10oz)

My favorite quiche, and a scrumptious new approach to "crust"-crispy, light & fabulous.

Chop and measure veggies in advance. Spray a 10" pie dish and both sides of tortillas with olive oil. For best results, use an oil mister, then a brush to spread oil evenly. Place tortillas in the dish in a circle so that they overlap slightly with at least an inch of each extending above the edge of dish. In a bowl, whisk eggs. Whisk in mayonnaise, milk, salt, pepper, coriander and nutmeg. Preheat oven to 350°. In a skillet, saute onion in grapeseed oil until soft. Add mushrooms, cook covered 4 minutes, stirring occasionally. Add spinach and stir 2-3 minutes. Remove from heat. Drain liquid. Stir spinach-mushroom mixture into egg mixture. Pour into tortilla crust and bake 30-35 minutes or until center is firm.

Egg & Sausage Bake

Serves 6-8 Corn Free

- 1¼ lb Yukon Gold potatoes, peeled and grated, equaling 2 cups
- 8 eggs
- 1¼ cups (10 oz) **light** coconut milk
- 1½ tsp sea salt
- 1 tsp onion powder
- 6 oz fully cooked, sliced chicken sausage*
- ¼ cup canned, diced green chiles (Use only with savory sausage), optional

This is a classic. Serve with Oat Pancakes, p.67, or the Blueberry Banana Muffins, p.71. This dish will draw a crowd at the breakfast table.

*Such as Trader Joe's® Sweet Apple Chicken Sausage or Aidells® Chicken & Apple, or, for a less sweet, more savory flavor, use garlic and herb chicken sausage from Trader Joe's® or a sausage with peppers.

Preheat oven to 350°. Brush or spray an 8x11 baking dish with grapeseed oil. Place the grated potatoes on 2 thicknesses of paper towels, wrap the towels around them and squeeze out excess liquid. Sometimes this needs to be done twice if the potatoes are especially watery. In a mixing bowl, whisk the eggs. Add the coconut milk, salt and onion powder, and the green chiles, if using, and whisk again. Stir in grated potatoes. Pour the potato-egg mixture into the baking dish. Scatter the sliced sausage over the egg mixture. Bake 25-30 minutes, or, if using a deeper baking dish, it may take an extra 5 minutes. The egg dish is ready when it feels firm in the center and a knife comes out clean. Allow to set for 5 minutes before serving.

Creamy Egg & Chile Casserole

Serves 6 Veg, Corn Free

- ¾ cup **whole** coconut milk
- ½ of 1-15oz can garbonzo beans, (almost 1 cup), drained well
- 1 tsp garlic powder
- 1⅛ tsp sea salt
- 1 Tbsp coconut flour
- 8 large eggs
- 1 7 oz can diced green chiles

Preheat oven to 325°. Generously brush or spray a 7x11 baking dish with grapeseed oil. Into a blender, pour the milk and beans. Blend on high 40 seconds or until smooth. Add the garlic powder, salt and flour, and blend 20 seconds. Add the eggs and blend on high 40 seconds. Stir in the chilies and pour into the baking dish. Bake 35 minutes or until the center is firm and the top is light golden brown. Cool 10 minutes and serve.

Everything goes into the blender. So easy and so good. We love this dish on Christmas morning. I make it the day before but only bake it 30 minutes, then bake it again 15 minutes or till heated through and firm in center. Can be doubled for a larger group. Wonderful with the Cinnamon Pecan Coffee Cake and Hot Fruit Compote (pp.67 & 79).

Berry Parfaits

Serves 4 Veg, V, Egg Free, Corn Free

- 1 13½ or 14 oz can **whole** coconut milk
- 1 Tbsp vanilla
- ¼ tsp liquid stevia
- 1 tsp xanthan gum
- ¾ cup blueberries
- ¾ cup strawberries
- ¾ cup blackberries
- ¾ cup raspberries

Berry Parfaits make a beautiful presentation for brunch or a lovely, light dessert for a summer evening dinner party. They are also wonderful with sliced peaches, kiwi or other fruits. Try a sprinkle of coconut.

Into a blender, pour the milk, vanilla, stevia and xanthan gum. Using the lowest speed, blend mixture together for 10 seconds. Scrape the sides of blender as needed. Blend on high 40 seconds. Pour into a 2 cup container, cover and chill 1-2 hours. Custard will continue to thicken as it chills. In four parfait glasses, create a layer of blueberries, followed by about 3 Tbsp of the custard, the strawberries, another 3 Tbsp of custard, the blackberries, another 3 Tbsp custard and the raspberries, or any other variation desired.

Coco Rum Fruit Salad

Makes 8 Servings Veg, V, Egg Free, Corn Free

Sauce

- 2½ Tbsp white rum
- 1½ Tbsp coconut palm sugar
- 1 cup **whole** coconut milk
- ¼ tsp liquid stevia
- ¼ tsp sea salt
- ⅛ tsp xanthan gum

- 2 cups fresh pineapple, cut in bite-sized pieces
- 2 cups fresh tangerine slices
- 2 cups red grapes
- 2 cups mango, cut in bite-sized pieces
- ⅓ cup unsweetened small flake coconut such as Bob's Red Mill®
- ⅓ cup unsweetened large flake coconut (Bob's Red Mill® or Let's Do Organic®)
- ⅓ cup slivered almonds, optional

A creamy, exotic twist for a pretty fruit salad. Or, a killer sauce for the Berry Parfaits, with or without the berries!

In a 1-qt saucepan, heat the rum and sugar on low 5 minutes without boiling, stirring occasionally. Cool in refrigerator 5 minutes. Into a blender, pour the rum with sugar, milk, stevia, salt and xanthan gum. Use the lowest speed on blender, such as "stir," for 10 seconds. Scrape the sides of blender and blend on high 40 seconds. Stir in the small flake coconut. Toss dressing with fruit, sprinkle with large flake coconut and almonds, if desired, and serve.

Hot Fruit Compote

Serves 10-12 Veg, V, Egg Free, Corn Free

- ½ cup water
- 2 cups dried apricots, halved
- 1½ cups fresh cranberries. washed and sorted
- 1 cup pitted, chopped dates
- ½ cup fresh grated zest of 1 large orange
- • the juice of the grated orange, about ¼ cup
- ¾ cup pitted prunes, halved
- 1½ cups fresh or frozen raspberries

Ideal as a warm side dish at breakfast or brunch, this Fruit Compote is also delicious as dessert with DF vanilla ice cream and my Shortbread cookies, p.129.

In a 3-qt saucepan, bring water, apricots, cranberries, and dates to a boil. Turn heat to low, cover and simmer, stirring occasionally, 5 minutes. Add orange zest, orange juice, prunes and raspberries. Stir and simmer another minute. Turn fruit mixture into a 1½-qt covered casserole or serving bowl and serve hot or store the casserole in refrigerator to reheat and serve again later. If reheating, heat oven to 350° and bake covered approximately 20 minutes, just until heated. The fruit compote is also delicious cold.

Millet "Oatmeal"

Makes 2 Servings Veg, V, Egg Free, Corn Free

- ½ cup millet
- 1½ cups water
- ¼ tsp sea salt, or to taste
- 2½ Tbsp coconut palm sugar or coconut nectar, to taste
- ½ tsp cinnamon
- • strawberries or any combination of berries, apples, pears, as desired
- • chopped walnuts or almonds, if desired

In a 1-qt saucepan, bring millet and water to a boil. Reduce heat and cook on low, uncovered, 25 minutes or until all water is absorbed. Remove from heat and add all remaining ingredients. Serve with plain or vanilla rice, almond or other DF "milk." Can be made ahead in a larger quantity without the fruit, and reheated, adding fruit.

For those who are oat-free, "oatmeal" is back on the menu! Millet, which has been around for thousands of years, has a toasted, nutty flavor and is high in nutrients such as B vitamins, folic acid, calcium, iron, potassium, magnesium and zinc. Especially Delightful, ¼ cup of millet provides 5.5g protein and 4.25g fiber, but only 189 calories.

Apple Cinnamon Granola

Makes 5⅓ Cups   Veg, V, Egg Free, Corn Free

- 2 cups soaked, baked steel cut oats, see p.11
- ⅓ cup whole buckwheat groats such as Pocono® brand*
- ¾ cup coarsely chopped raw almonds
- 1 cup coarsely chopped raw walnuts
- 1 cup coarsely chopped unsulfured, unsweetened dried apple
- ⅓ cup raisins, optional
- ¼ cup water
- ½ cup coconut palm sugar
- 1 Tbsp + 2 tsp cinnamon
- ½ tsp sea salt

*If you can't find whole buckwheat groats, Pocono® or Bob's Red Mill® makes a suitable creamy buckwheat hot cereal that can be substituted.

One of the things I missed when I started eating "clean" was granola. Store bought, and even homemade recipes, use rolled oats (see p.136) and most are full of refined sugar. As sweet & crunchy as mine is, it's also wholesome and low in natural sugar.

Preheat oven to 275°. Spray a jelly roll pan generously with grapeseed oil. In a bowl, mix the oats, buckwheat, nuts, apple and raisins, if using them. In a 1-qt saucepan, heat the water on low heat. Add the sugar and stir 2-3 minutes until sugar has dissolved completely. Remove from heat. Stir in the cinnamon and salt. Pour this mixture over the dry ingredients and stir several minutes until the oat mixture is coated completely. Spread evenly on baking sheet and bake 20 minutes. Cool on pan 15 minutes, then loosen with a spatula. Granola gets crunchier as it cools.

Nutty Molasses Granola

Makes 4 Cups   Veg, V, Egg Free, Corn Free

- 2 cups soaked, baked steel cut oats, see p.11
- 1 cup raw almonds, whole or halved
- ¾ cup raw walnuts, halved
- ¼ cup raw or toasted sunflower seeds
- 2 Tbsp toasted flaxseeds, whole
- ¼ cup water
- ½ cup coconut palm sugar
- 2 Tbsp blackstrap molasses
- 12 drops liquid stevia
- ⅛ tsp sea salt

Low in sugar, high in nutrients and flavor. A real treat as a snack or tasty added crunch to oatmeal. It is the secret of the scrumptious Molasses Stuffed Acorn Squash on p.115.

Preheat oven to 275°. Brush or spray a jelly roll pan generously with grapeseed oil. In a large bowl, mix the first 5 ingredients. In a 1-qt saucepan, heat the water on low heat. Add the sugar and stir 2-3 minutes until sugar has disolved completely. Remore from heat. Stir in the molasses, stevia and salt. Pour over the dry ingredients and mix thoroughly. Spread evenly on baking sheet and bake 20 minutes. Cool on pan 15 minutes and then loosen with a spatula before allowing it to finish cooling.

Soups

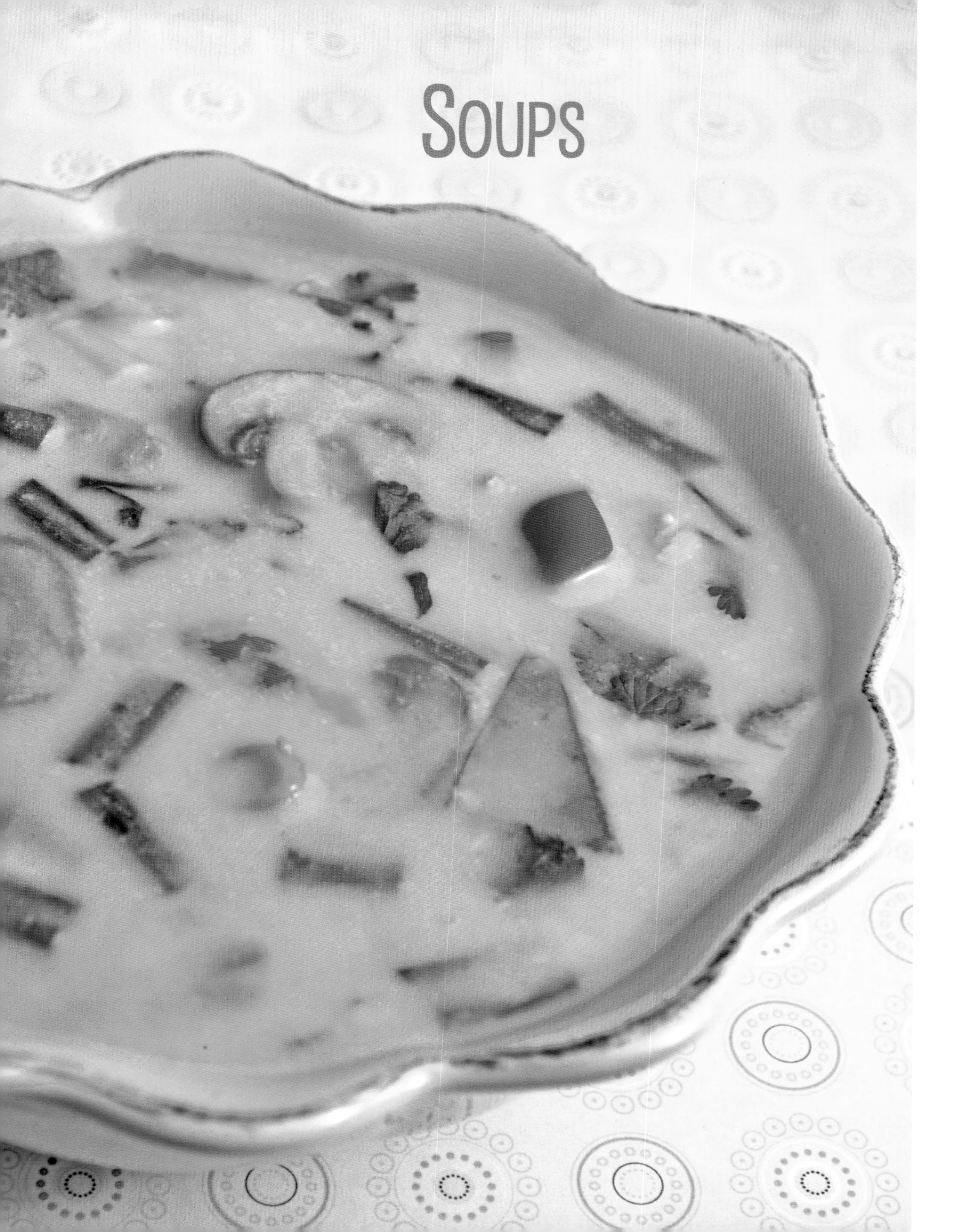

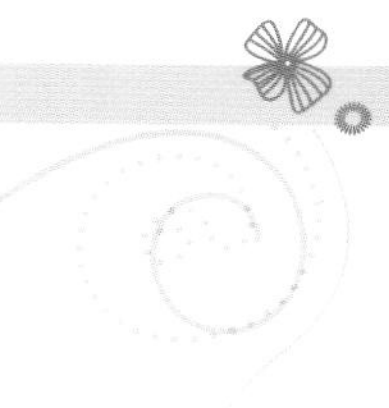

Coconut Curry Soup

Serves 7-8 Egg Free, Corn Free

- 32 oz chicken stock or broth
- 2 medium boneless, skinless chicken breasts, whole
- 2-2½ Tbsp sliced lemon grass, optional but delicious!
- 1 medium brown onion, chopped about 2 cups
- ⅓ lb sliced brown mushrooms, about 8-9
- 5 green onions, sliced in ½" pieces
- 1 medium red bell pepper, chopped
- 6 Tbsp lemon juice
- ½ tsp ground ginger
- 1 tsp garlic powder
- ¾ tsp red chili pepper
- 1 tsp curry powder
- 1¾ tsp sea salt
- ¾ cup cilantro, chopped and moderately packed
- 2 medium tomatoes, chopped, about 1½ cups
- 2½ cups (or about 1½ cans) **light** coconut milk
- 3 Tbsp coconut palm sugar

The flavors and colors in this soup are fabulous! Tangy, sweet and sour, in a warm and exotic blend of savory goodness that delights the senses. This is definitely a meal in itself.

It is helpful to have all the ingredients chopped and measured before beginning. This way, the vegetables won't be overcooked at the end. In a 6-qt soup pot, bring the chicken stock to a boil. Lower heat to medium and then cook the chicken breasts and lemon grass in the chicken stock, covered 15 minutes. Remove the chicken to a cutting board. Cut chicken into bite-sized pieces and return to the pot. Add the brown onion, cover and cook on medium heat 4 minutes. Add mushrooms, green onion and bell pepper. Cook another 3-4 minutes. Stir in the lemon juice, ginger, garlic powder, red chili pepper, curry powder and salt. Next, add the cilantro and tomatoes and cook 2 more minutes. Stir in the coconut milk and sugar. Serve as soon as the soup is piping hot.

Creamy Carrot Soup

Serves 8 Veg & V (substitute vegetable broth), Egg Free, Corn Free

- 2½ Tbsp ghee, divided: 1½ Tbsp + 1 Tbsp
- 2 cups chopped brown onion
- 32 oz chicken stock or broth
- 2 lb carrots (about 10-12 large), peeled and cut into 2" chunks
- 3 cups water
- ¾ lb Yukon Gold potatoes, peeled and cut into 2" chunks
- 1 tsp sea salt
- ⅛-¼ tsp white pepper, to taste
- 2 Tbsp fresh parsley or 1 Tbsp fresh dill, chopped for garnish, optional

Creamy and elegant, wonderful with Seeded Quick Bread on p.59 or Rosemary Rolls, p.61. This soup is also lovely with Layered Herbs & Cream, p.119.

In a 6-qt soup pot, cook the onion in 1½ Tbsp ghee until soft, about 10 minutes. Add the stock or broth and carrots, and bring to a boil. Reduce heat, cover and simmer until carrots are very tender, about 30 minutes. Meanwhile, in a smaller pot, bring 3 cups of water to a boil. Add the potatoes, cover and simmer 20-25 minutes until soft. Pour the carrot stock mixture through a strainer over a bowl in order to reserve the stock. Transfer ½ of the carrots to blender or food processor. Add 1 cup of reserved stock, blend until smooth and pour back into the soup pot. Repeat with the other ½ of carrots and 1 cup of reserved stock. Pour into soup pot. After pouring the potatoes through the same strainer and disposing of the water, add potatoes to blender with remaining stock. Add 1 Tbsp ghee and blend until smooth. Pour into soup pot. Add salt and pepper. Heat, if necessary, on low. Garnish with parsley or dill, and serve.

Cream of Broc & Cauli Soup

Serves 7 Veg & V (substitute vegetable broth), Egg Free, Corn Free

- 1½ lb broccoli, not including stems
- 2 lb cauliflower, not including stems
- 4 cups water
- 2 14½ oz cans of chicken stock or broth
- ½ cup plain rice or almond milk
- 1 Tbsp olive oil
- ¼ tsp sea salt
- • dash of nutmeg, optional

Creamy as this soup seems, there is not a drop of cream in it. In fact, this vitamin and phytonutrient rich soup is basically vegetables & broth. At about 100 calories per serving, it delivers about 6g fiber, 5½g protein and 700mg potassium, all with only about 2½g of fat.

Cut washed broccoli and cauliflower into 2-3" chunks, discarding stems. In a 6-qt pot, bring water and cauliflower to a boil. Reduce heat to medium, cover and cook cauliflower 5 minutes. Add broccoli and cover. Cook another 10 minutes until both broccoli and cauliflower are soft. Drain all water and transfer ½ the broccoli and cauli solids to a blender or food processor. Add 1 cup of the chicken broth to blender, cover and blend on high. You may need to use a large spoon to push the vegetables down to be blended. Add remaining ½ of vegetables and blend 2-3 minutes to be sure that the mixture is very smooth. Pour mixture from blender back into the pot. Stir in remaining chicken broth, milk, olive oil and salt. Heat on low and serve with a dash of nutmeg, if using.

Creamy Lemon Chicken Soup

Serves 8 Corn Free

- 46-48 oz chicken stock or broth
- 2 tsp fresh minced parsley
- 2 tsp fresh chives, chopped + 1-2 Tbsp for garnish
- 2 tsp grated lemon zest
- 1 large boneless, skinless chicken breast, cut into 3 pieces
- 4 large eggs
- 6 Tbsp fresh lemon juice
- 2 cups cooked brown rice

Light, creamy lemon and savory chicken with chives create a flavorful, aromatic soup. It is lovely as a first course, yet hearty enough for a whole meal.

In a 6-qt pot, bring chicken stock, parsley, chives and lemon zest to a boil. Add the chicken, cover, lower heat and simmer 15 minutes. Remove from heat. Remove chicken to a cutting board and chop finely, cover and set aside. In a bowl, whisk the eggs. Add the lemon juice and whisk again. **Slowly** pour several cups of broth into the bowl, stirring constantly. Broth should be added to egg mixture very slowly to keep the eggs from curdling. While pot is still removed from heat, return this mixture very slowly to the remaining broth, stirring constantly. Add the rice and chicken, and cook over medium-low heat, stirring constantly 4-6 minutes or until soup thickens very slightly. **Do not** let soup boil or the eggs will curdle. Serve garnished with additional chives. The soup may be made ahead and reheated over low heat, being careful not to let it boil.

Tortilla Soup

Serves 8-10 Veg & V (substitute vegetable broth, no chicken), Egg Free

- 2 qt (64 oz) chicken stock or broth
- 2 medium-size skinless, boneless chicken breasts
- ⅓ cup dry lentils
- ½ cup lightly packed, fresh cilantro leaves
- 3 cloves garlic, minced, or ¾ tsp garlic powder
- 3 Tbsp chili powder
- 3 Tbsp dehydrated onion (Do not substitute fresh)
- ½ tsp cumin
- 1 tsp sea salt
- 2 15 oz cans black beans, drained
- 1 14½ oz can diced tomatoes, undrained
- ⅔ cup fresh corn kernels, or frozen
- 1-2 avocados, diced
- 1-2 brown rice tortillas for tortilla chips, recipe p.123

Warm and satisfying, with a Mexican flair, Tortilla Soup is delicioso! Even without chicken, this tasty soup is still high in protein thanks to the lentils and black beans.

In a 6-qt soup pot, bring the chicken stock to a boil. Add the chicken breasts whole and reduce heat to medium. Cover and simmer 15 minutes, just until chicken is no longer pink in center. Turn off heat and remove the chicken to a cutting board. Turn heat to high, bring to a boil and add the lentils. Return to boil, and turn heat down, cover and let lentils cook 10 minutes. Shred or cut chicken to bite-sized pieces. Cover and set chicken aside to add back in later. Add remaining ingredients, except for the corn, avocados and tortillas. The lentils should be almost cooked. Add the corn and chicken, and cook on medium-low 4 minutes. Remove from heat. Ladle soup into bowls and garnish with avocado and tortilla chips.

Chipotle Meatball Soup

Serves 8-10 Egg Free, Corn Free

Smoky chipotle in a hearty soup of spicy meatballs and black beans is a satisfying meal complete with dark green vegetables and all of the goodness of legumes.

- 24 chipotle meatballs, recipe p.15
- 64 oz chicken stock or broth
- 1 large yellow or brown onion, chopped, about 3 cups
- 4 cups chopped kale, moderately packed, about 5 leaves
- 3 large cloves garlic, chopped
- 8 oz tomato sauce
- 3 medium tomatoes, chopped, or 1 14.5 oz can tomatoes, undrained
- 1 tsp sea salt
- ½-1 tsp smoked chipotle chili powder, to taste
- ⅔ cup cooked brown rice
- 1 15 oz can black beans, drained

In a 6-qt soup pot, bring the chicken stock or broth to a boil. Add the onion, kale and garlic. Cover, reduce heat to medium-low, and cook 15 minutes. Stir in the tomato sauce, tomatoes, salt, chipotle chili powder, rice, beans and meatballs. Cover and simmer just until heated through. Serve immediately.

Italian Wedding Soup

Serves 10 Egg Free, Corn Free

Soup always sounds good in the winter months. This hearty Italian soup is quick and easy to make but tastes like you spent the day preparing it. My Rosemary Rolls are perfect with it.

- 5 cups water
- 1 cup brown rice shell pasta (I like Tinkyada® brand)
- 1½ 15 oz cans black beans, undrained
- 12-14 oz fully cooked sweet Italian style chicken sausage such as Trader Joe's® brand, casings removed and sliced, or Italian Meatballs p.15
- ½ tsp sea salt
- 2-3 cloves garlic, minced
- 2 Tbsp fresh basil leaves, chopped or 1¾ tsp dried basil
- 3 large tomatoes, chopped or 1 15 oz can diced tomatoes, undrained
- 6 oz fresh spinach, about 3-4 cups, lightly packed

In a 6-qt pot, bring water to a boil and add pasta. Turn heat down to a low boil and cook pasta about 10 minutes, just until al dente, but not soft. Turn heat down to a simmer. Add black beans, sausage or meatballs, salt, garlic and basil. Cook covered 5 minutes, stirring occasionally. Add tomatoes and spinach. Cover and simmer another 3 minutes. Serve garnished with a sprinkle of chopped fresh basil.

Salads

Balsamic Rice & Bean Salad

Makes 3 Entree Salads or 7-8 Sides   Veg, V, Egg Free, Corn Free

- 1½ cups cooked brown rice
- 1½ cups navy or cannellini beans, cooked from dry or canned, rinsed and drained
- 1 cup chopped celery
- 1¼ cups chopped yellow or orange bell pepper (about 1 large pepper)
- ⅓ cup chopped green onion
- ½ cup fresh basil leaves, torn or chopped
- 1 cup halved cherry or egg tomatoes
- 1 cup Balsamic Dressing, or more to taste
- ⅔ cup chopped walnuts and/or pumpkin seeds, optional

Lots of crunch and flavor. This salad is even more tasty the next day and it's also a great topper for a green salad. Beans (aka legumes) are a very important part of healthy eating. There are many varieties to choose from. In a ½ cup of navy beans, you get about 9g protein and 6g fiber with less than 1g fat.

Balsamic Vinaigrette Dressing (Makes 2¼ cups)

- ½ cup red wine vinegar
- ½ cup balsamic vinegar
- 1 cup grapeseed oil
- ¼ tsp sea salt
- 1½ Tbsp coconut palm sugar
- 1 small clove garlic, pressed, or ¼ tsp garlic powder
- ½ tsp ground mustard
- ¼ cup water
- • pinch paprika
- ¼ tsp + ⅛ tsp xanthan gum
- 8 drops liquid stevia, optional

Shake all dressing ingredients, except xanthan gum, together in a jar with a tight-fitting lid. Add the xanthan gum and shake again. For smoother flavors, emulsify the dressing by mixing all ingredients, except xanthan gum, in a blender on high for 30 seconds. Add the xanthan gum and blend again for 10 seconds. Store in refrigerator.

In a large bowl, combine all ingredients, except for walnuts and pumpkin seeds, if using. Toss together with a cup or more of dressing. The nuts or seeds can be sprinkled on top when the salad is served or mixed in.

Grilled Basil Shrimp & Chicken Salad

Makes 2 Entree Salads   Egg Free, Corn Free

- • a bed of your favorite greens
- 2-4 Tbsp, or as much as desired, fresh basil leaves, torn
- 4-6 oz shrimp and/or chicken from the Grilled Basil Shrimp & Chicken, recipe p.39
- • several pieces of red bell pepper from the same recipe
- 2-3 spoonfuls cooked millet or amaranth from the same recipe
- 4-6 pitted kalamata olives, halved
- • thinly sliced red onion, to taste
- • dollop of hummus, recipe p.123

Basil Oregano Dressing

- ¼ cup olive oil
- ½ cup grapeseed oil
- ¼ cup **white** balsamic vinegar
- 2 Tbsp red wine vinegar
- 1½ tsp dried oregano
- 2½ tsp dried basil
- 1½ tsp sea salt
- 1¼ tsp garlic powder
- ⅛ tsp xanthan gum

Your choice. Make it with shrimp and chicken, or just your favorite. A nice way to use the leftover shrimp or chicken and bell peppers from a previous dinner of Grilled Basil Shrimp & Chicken!

Shake all dressing ingredients in a jar with a tight-fitting lid. Store in refrigerator. Toss all ingredients, including dressing, or assemble the ingredients atop the bed of greens and serve with the Basil Oregano Dressing.

Classic BBQ Chicken Salad

Makes 4-6 Entree Salads   Egg Free

- 1 medium head romaine lettuce or equivalent favorite salad greens
- ⅓ cup jicama, thinly sliced or grated
- ½ cup shredded carrots
- ½ cup chopped red onion
- 1 cup small egg tomatoes, halved, or other chopped tomatoes
- 1 cup fresh corn, or frozen or canned, drained
- 1½ cups black beans, rinsed and drained
- 2-3 BBQ'd chicken breasts (BBQ sauce p.103), cut into bite-sized pieces
- 1½ cups avocado, chopped
- ½ cup fresh cilantro leaves

BBQ Ranch Dressing

See recipe bottom of p.97

During summer, we use the BBQ a lot. I always grill extra chicken so that we can enjoy this salad a night or two later.

In a large bowl, toss chopped lettuce, jicama, carrots, onion, tomatoes, corn and black beans. Divide salad into 4-6 large salad bowls. Top with chicken, avocado and cilantro. Pour BBQ ranch dressing over salads and serve. Or, toss all ingredients, including dressing, together in the large bowl and serve. We love extra BBQ sauce drizzled on top.

Tabouli with Quinoa

Makes 6-8 Servings   Veg, V, Egg Free, Corn Free

- 1 cup uncooked quinoa
- ¼ cup olive oil
- ½ cup lemon juice
- 2 large cloves garlic, minced, or 2½ tsp garlic powder
- 1¾ tsp sea salt
- 1 large cucumber, unpeeled, diced, about 2½ cups
- 1 large or 2 medium tomatoes, diced, about 1½ cups
- ½ cup sliced black olives
- ¼ cup sliced green onions
- 1 cup fresh Italian flat leaf parsley, chopped
- ¾ cup fresh mint, chopped

When I take this Tabouli With Quinoa to a party, it's a hit! Also nice, is that it tastes even better the next day, so I make it ahead of time and have one less thing to do on the big day.

Rinse and drain quinoa. In a 2-qt saucepan bring quinoa and 2 cups water to a boil. Reduce heat, cover and simmer 15 minutes, or until all the water is absorbed. Cool quinoa in refrigerator until chilled. In a large bowl, thoroughly mix the olive oil, lemon juice, garlic and salt into quinoa. Stir in the cucumber, tomatoes, olives, green onions, parsley and mint until well combined. Garnish with mint or parsley. Serve room temperature or chilled.

Greek Salad

Makes 4 Entree Salads or 6-8 Sides   Veg, V, Egg Free, Corn Free

- 2½ cups cucumber, unpeeled and chopped into ½" pieces
- 2½ cups Roma tomatoes or garden variety, chopped into ½" pieces
- 2½ cups garbanzo beans, drained
- ½ cup or more thinly sliced red onion
- ¼ cup fresh dill, chopped
- ¼ cup fresh Italian flat leaf parsley, chopped

Greek Dressing

- ⅓ cup olive oil
- ⅓ cup sunflower oil or grapeseed oil
- ⅓ cup + 1 tsp lemon juice
- 1 Tbsp apple cider vinegar
- 1 clove garlic, pressed, or ½ tsp garlic powder
- ¾ tsp sea salt, or to taste
- 2 tsp dried dill weed
- 1¼ tsp dried tarragon
- 1/16 tsp xanthan gum

Shake all dressing ingredients together in a jar with a tight-fitting lid. For smoother flavors, emulsify the dressing by mixing ingredients in a blender on high 30 seconds. Combine all salad ingredients in a large bowl. Toss with dressing and refrigerate at least 4 hours or overnight.

The creaminess of garbanzo beans becomes a tasty exchange for the cheese usually used in a Greek Salad. Even better the second day, it's best made a day ahead, which makes it twice as convenient for you.

Crab Salad with Mustard Dressing

Makes 4 Entree Salads Corn Free

- 1 small head bok choy, about 2 lb, chopped
- ¾ cup shredded carrots
- 1 cup egg tomatoes, halved, or 1 cup chopped tomatoes
- 3 green onions, sliced
- 12-16 oz fresh cooked crab meat or container of prepared crab
- 3 hard boiled eggs, sliced

Creamy Mustard Dressing

- 1 cup soy-free mayonnaise such as Soy-Free Vegenaise®
- ½ cup deli-style mustard with horseradish
- ½ cup prepared mustard
- ¼ cup water to thin dressing to the right consistency

This special salad is Delightful for a luncheon. Pair it with Harvest Pumpkin Bread on p.63 or Latte Muffins p.65.

Whisk all dressing ingredients or shake in a jar with a tight-fitting lid. In a small bowl, mix crab with ¼ cup of dressing, or to taste. In a large bowl, toss bok choy, carrots, tomatoes and green onions. Add desired amount of dressing and toss again. Divide salad into bowls. Put a scoop of crab meat on each and garnish with sliced egg.

BBQ Black Bean Salad

Makes 2 Entree Salads Veg

- 2 15 oz cans black beans, rinsed and drained on a paper towel
- 1½ cups small egg tomatoes, halved, or other chopped tomatoes
- ½ cup fresh, frozen or canned corn kernels (Trader Joe's® frozen roasted corn is great)
- ½ cup fresh cilantro leaves
- 3 green onions, sliced
- 1½ cups chopped jicama
- 3 hard boiled eggs, shelled and chopped

BBQ Ranch Dressing

- ¼ cup BBQ Sauce with Natural Sweeteners, p.103
- 1 cup soy-free mayonnaise such as Soy-Free Vegenaise®
- ⅓ cup plain rice or almond milk
- ½ tsp cider vinegar
- ½ tsp dill weed
- ¼ tsp sea salt

A taste of summer, this salad makes a great entree or can be used as a side. It is a natural with the Cornbread on p.57. Combine this tangy BBQ sauce with the dressing, as directed, or drizzle it over the top of the salad as pictured. Both ways are delicious.

For dressing, mix all of the ingredients together in a jar with a tight-fitting lid, and shake. For salad, combine first 6 ingredients in a large bowl. Shake the dressing well before pouring desired amount over salad. Toss salad and confirm that you have the correct amount of dressing. Add the boiled eggs, toss gently and serve.

Tangy Bok Choy Salad

Makes 4 Entree Salads

Egg Free, Corn Free

- 1 large head of bok choy
- 8 green onions, sliced
- 1 8 oz can water chestnuts, drained and sliced
- ¾ cup fresh cilantro leaves, lightly packed
- 2 11 oz cans mandarin oranges, drained
- 2 cups cooked chicken, cut into bite-sized pieces
- ½ cup slivered almonds, toasted

Sweet & Tangy Asian Dressing

- ½ cup seasoned rice vinegar (I use Marukan® or Nakano®)
- ¾ cup grapeseed oil
- 3½ Tbsp coconut palm sugar
- 1 tsp sea salt
- 1¼ tsp black pepper

Shake all dressing ingredients together in a jar with a tight-fitting lid. Slice bok choy lengthwise, then widthwise into bite-sized pieces. Toss all salad ingredients, except for almonds, in a large mixing bowl. Shake the dressing well and pour desired amount over the salad. Sprinkle with almonds and serve.

A tangy, sweet change-up on a crunchy, fresh salad. Serve with my Seeded Quick Bread p.59, or Pumpkin Spice Muffins p.71.

Broccoli BBQ Salad (can be made with chicken)

Makes 4 Entree Salads or 6-8 Sides

Veg, V, Egg Free, Corn Free

- 4-5 cups broccoli flowerets, about 2 lb before removing stems, cut in 1" bite-sized pieces
- 1 15 oz can black beans, rinsed and drained
- 1 cup cooked brown rice
- 1½ cups cherry tomatoes, halved, or 3 medium tomatoes, chopped
- 1 cup red onion, chopped
- ¾ cup fresh cilantro leaves, lightly packed
- 2 chicken breasts BBQ'd in naturally sweetened BBQ sauce, optional

BBQ Ranch Dressing

- ¼ cup BBQ Sauce with Natural Sweeteners, p.103
- 1 cup soy-free mayonnaise such as Soy-Free Vegenaise®
- ⅓ cup plain rice or almond milk
- ½ tsp cider vinegar
- ½ tsp dill weed
- ¼ tsp sea salt

Did you know that a cup of raw broccoli has only 31 calories and ⅓ g total fat? It has no measurable saturated, monounsaturated or polyunsaturated fats. It has 2g dietary fiber, 3g protein and only 2g sugar. More to cheer about, broccoli provides the phytonutrients that fight diseases like cancer. It increases immunity and aids in healthy heart function by interfering with the negative impact of LDL cholesterol.

For dressing, mix all ingredients together in a jar with a tight-fitting lid, and shake. If using barbecued chicken or tofu, cut into bite-sized pieces, cover and set aside in the refrigerator. In a large bowl, combine broccoli, black beans, rice, tomatoes, onion and cilantro. Add the chicken or tofu, if using, and dressing to the broccoli mixture. Toss and serve.

Chickpea Salad

Makes 2 Entree Salads or 5-6 Sides

Veg, V, Egg Free, Corn Free

- 2 14 oz cans garbanzo beans, drained
- 1 cup chopped red bell pepper
- 1 cup chopped yellow bell pepper
- 1½ cups peeled and chopped carrots
- ½ cup chopped yellow onion
- ¼ cup fresh Italian flat leaf parsley
- ⅓ cup toasted sunflower seeds
- ½ cup dried, unsweetened or naturally sweetened cranberries

Dressing

- ¼ cup olive oil
- ½ cup grapeseed oil
- ½ cup red wine vinegar
- 2 cloves garlic, pressed, or 1 tsp garlic powder
- 1¼ tsp sea salt
- ½ tsp black pepper
- ¼ tsp cumin

Shake all dressing ingredients together in a jar with a tight-fitting lid. Combine all salad ingredients. Add desired amount of dressing. Toss and serve. Reserve the sunflower seeds and cranberries if not serving right away.

This zesty salad is colorful, crunchy & protein-packed. Couple it with the Banana Bread sans the chocolate chips on p.63, or with the Seeded Quick Bread on p.59, using the sweeter variation suggested below the recipe.

Quinoa with Dried Cherries & Pistachios

Makes 4-5 Entree Salads or 12-14 Sides

Veg, V, Egg Free, Corn Free

- 1¾ cups uncooked red quinoa
- 2 cups chopped brown onion
- 2 Tbsp grapeseed oil
- 2 cups water
- ½ cup lemon juice
- ⅔ cup dry white wine
- 3 Tbsp olive oil
- 10 drops liquid stevia
- 2 tsp sea salt
- ½ tsp freshly ground black pepper
- 2 cups cooked green lentils
- 1½ cups cooked cannellini or great northern navy beans
- 1-2 cups thinly sliced celery
- ½ cup fresh Italian flat leaf parsley, chopped
- ½ cup fresh mint leaves, chopped
- 1 cup unsweetened dried sweet cherries
- 1 cup toasted pistachios

So colorful and so much flavor. Did you know that quinoa is actually a seed? Isn't it Delightful that eating a "clean," nutritious mix of wholesome seeds, lentils, beans, nuts, fresh herbs and vegetables is also so delicious?

Rinse and drain quinoa. In a 3-qt saucepan, cook onion in the grapeseed oil on medium-high heat 6 minutes, just until tender. Add the water and bring to a boil. Add quinoa and return to a boil. Lower heat and simmer covered 15-18 minutes, until quinoa is tender and water is absorbed. Remove from heat and cool slightly. For dressing, whisk the lemon juice, wine, olive oil, stevia, salt and pepper in a small bowl. In a large bowl, combine the lentils, beans and celery with the quinoa and add the lemon wine dressing. Stir in parsley, mint, cherries and pistachios. Toss gently and serve warm, room temperature, or chilled.

Balsamic Vinaigrette Dressing

Makes 2¼ Cups Veg, V, Egg Free, Corn Free

- ½ cup red wine vinegar
- ½ cup balsamic vinegar
- 1 cup grapeseed oil
- ¼ tsp sea salt
- 1½ Tbsp coconut palm sugar
- 1 small clove garlic, pressed, or ¼ tsp garlic powder
- ½ tsp ground mustard
- ¼ cup water
- • pinch paprika
- ¼ tsp + ⅛ tsp xanthan gum
- 8 drops liquid stevia, optional

Why make your own salad dressings? We obviously want dressings that are GF, DF and SF. You can put a "Check" in that box. These dressings are full of herbs and healthy ingredients in a wide range of flavors. But, in addition to that, consider that my dressings contain no nitrates, nitrites, high fructose corn syrup, hydrolyzed corn protein, MSG, sodium benzoate or bisulfate, maltodextrin...you get the picture. I like to save bottles with nice flip-top spouts or tight-fitting lids to use for my salad dressings or BBQ sauce.

Pour all ingredients, except xanthan gum, into a jar with a tight-fitting lid and shake well. Add xanthan gum and shake again. For smoother flavors, emulsify the dressing by mixing all ingredients, except xanthan gum, in a blender on high 30 seconds. Add xanthan gum and blend again 10 seconds. Store in refrigerator.

"Buttermilk" Ranch Dressing

Makes 1⅓ Cups Veg, V, Egg Free, Corn Free

- 1 cup soy-free mayonnaise such as Soy-Free Vegenaise®
- ⅓ cup plain rice or almond milk
- ½ tsp cider vinegar
- ½ tsp dill weed
- ¼ tsp sea salt
- 1/32 tsp xanthan gum (this is ¼ of ⅛ tsp and all you need)

Pour all ingredients into a jar with a tight-fitting lid and shake well. Store in refrigerator.

Creamy Mustard Dressing

Makes 2¼ Cups Veg, V, Egg Free, Corn Free

- 1 cup soy-free mayonnaise such as Soy-Free Vegenaise®
- ½ cup deli-style mustard with horseradish
- ½ cup prepared mustard
- ¼ cup water

Whisk all four ingredients or shake them in a jar with a tight-fighting lid. Store in refrigerator.

Sweet & Tangy Asian Dressing 1¼ Cups (See p.99)

Italian Dressing

Makes 1½ Cups — Veg, V, Egg Free, Corn Free

- ¼ cup olive oil
- ½ cup grapeseed oil
- ¾ cup red wine vinegar
- 1 clove garlic, pressed, or 1 tsp garlic powder
- 1¼ tsp sea salt
- ¾ tsp black pepper
- 4½ tsp fresh oregano leaves, or 2 tsp dried
- ¼ tsp xanthan gum

Blend all ingredients, except xanthan gum, 30 seconds in blender. Add xanthan gum. Blend 10 seconds. Store in refrigerator.

Basil Oregano Dressing

Makes 1 Cup, easily doubled — Veg, V, Egg Free, Corn Free

- ¼ cup olive oil
- ½ cup grapeseed oil
- ¼ cup **white** balsamic vinegar
- 2 Tbsp red wine vinegar
- 1½ tsp dried oregano
- 2½ tsp dried basil
- 1½ tsp sea salt
- 1¼ tsp garlic powder
- ¼ tsp xanthan gum

Shake all ingredients together in a jar with a tight-fitting lid. Store in refrigerator.

BBQ Sauce with Natural Sweeteners

Makes 3 Cups (24 oz) — Veg, V, Egg Free, Corn Free

- 2 6 oz cans natural, unsweetened tomato paste
- 1 small clove garlic, pressed, or ½ tsp garlic powder
- 1½ Tbsp apple cider vinegar
- ¼ cup + 1 Tbsp blackstrap molasses
- ⅔ cup coconut palm sugar
- 1 Tbsp olive oil
- 1⅓ cup water, or more for desired thickness
- 1½ tsp sea salt
- 1/16-⅛ tsp cayenne pepper, or to taste
- ¼ tsp GF hickory seasoning liquid smoke, such as Wright's®

In a 3-qt saucepan, combine all ingredients using a whisk. Simmer 10 minutes, stirring often. Pour into a 26 oz jar. Store in refrigerator up to 1 month.

The use of high fructose corn syrup is out of control. It is found in just about every processed, packaged food. HFCS is a big problem in BBQ sauce. It is usually the second listed ingredient, which makes it one of the main ingredients. This is because it's sweeter and cheaper than sucrose (table sugar). A highly refined, processed sugar striped of any nutrition and very high in calories (4 per gram), the biggest problem with HFCS is its metabolism. Studies show HFCS to be linked to and, in part, responsible for the alarming increase of heart and kidney disease, obesity, type 2 diabetes and other diseases.* So, here's my answer...homemade BBQ sauce.

* Metabolic Danger of High-Fructose Corn Syrup, Life Extension Magazine, December 2008.

Greek Dressing 1⅓ Cups (See p.95)

Vegetables, Rice & Sides

Indian Style Veggies

Makes 6-8 Sides Veg, V, Egg Free, Corn Free

- 1½ Tbsp coconut oil
- 1 small red onion, sliced, about 1½ cups
- ½ small head cauliflower, cut into bite-sized pieces
- 1½ cups peeled and cubed Yukon Gold potatoes
- 1-2 Tbsp water
- 1 sliced orange bell pepper, about 1 cup
- 2 cloves garlic, chopped
- 3 cups broccoli, cut into bite-sized pieces
- ½ cup **light** coconut milk
- 1¼ tsp sea salt
- ⅛ tsp cayenne pepper, to taste
- 2½ tsp curry powder
- ⅛ tsp liquid stevia
- 1 Tbsp coconut palm sugar
- ⅔ cup cooked lentils

This vegetable medley spices up an ordinary dinner while providing a wide array of essential vitamins, minerals and phytonutrients. This recipe makes a lot, which is a bonus because it's delicious served chilled another day as a salad.

In a skillet, saute the onion, cauliflower and potato in the oil 4 minutes on medium-high heat, covered when not stirring. If necessary, add 1-2 Tbsp water. Add the bell pepper and garlic, and cook another 3-4 minutes. Stir in the broccoli, coconut milk, salt, cayenne pepper, curry powder, stevia and sugar. Cover to cook about 5 minutes, just until the vegetables are tender-crisp. Stir in the cooked lentils, heat and serve.

Baked Yam Fries (Photo p.18)

Makes 4 Servings Veg, V, Egg Free, Corn Free

- 2 large yams, peeled
- 1 Tbsp olive oil
- ¼ tsp garlic powder
- ½ tsp sea salt

If yams have been refrigerated, remove and allow 30 minutes before preparing. This makes them much easier to slice. Preheat oven to 375°. Spray a baking sheet with olive oil. Slice yams into ⅓" thick rounds. If desired, slice again lengthwise into 2-3" lengths resembling traditional french fries. A French fry cutter is helpful for this. Toss yams in a large bowl with the oil. Sprinkle with garlic powder and salt, and toss again. Spread yams out evenly on a baking sheet so that pieces do not touch. Bake 8-10 minutes. Flip yams with a fork or spatula and spread evenly. Bake another 6-8 minutes or until they are browning and softened to your preference. Enjoy!

No deep frying necessary for these tasty "fries." But they hit the spot just as well, and while they taste like a big splurge, yams are a beneficial "health food." In one medium yam, there are about 260 calories, no fat, 9g fiber, 3g protein, 1,521mg potassium, and almost a third of the recommended daily value of calcium.

Zucchini Marinara

Makes 4 Entrees or 8 Sides   Veg, V, Egg Free, Corn Free

- 3 lb zucchini, sliced lengthwise or in rounds, ¼" thick
- • olive oil
- • sea salt
- ½ of 1 yellow or brown onion, sliced thin
- 3-4 cloves garlic, chopped
- ½ recipe of Old World Tomato Basil Marinara, p.45

We like this so much we sometimes eat it in lieu of spaghetti. Serve with Rosemary Rolls on p.61. Delicious!

Preheat oven to 400°. Brush a baking sheet with olive oil (you may need 2 baking sheets). Working on the baking sheet, mix the onion slices and garlic in the olive oil. Add the sliced zucchini and brush both sides so that they are coated. Sprinkle with sea salt. Roast uncovered 6 minutes. Remove from the oven and turn each piece over. Return to oven another 6 minutes. Remove from the oven and arrange zucchini and onions on a platter. Pour Tomato Basil Marinara over and garnish with some of the onion.

Kale & Onions

Serves 4-6   Veg, V, Egg Free, Corn Free

- 1 medium red onion, sliced and halved
- 2 Tbsp olive oil, divided: 1 Tbsp + 1 Tbsp
- 3 cloves garlic, chopped
- 1½ lb kale with stems, stems removed and rough chopped
- 1-1¼ tsp sea salt, to taste
- 1½ tsp red wine, optional

A savory complement to chicken or fish. Lots of flavor and full of the phytonutrients and benefits of dark, leafy green vegetables, but still very low in calories, fat & cholesterol.

In a skillet, saute the onion in 1 Tbsp olive oil 5 minutes on medium-low heat, cover when not stirring. Add 1 more Tbsp olive oil, 1 Tbsp water, garlic and kale. Stir and cook on medium heat about 10 minutes or until kale is soft, covering when not stirring. Add salt and the wine, if desired.

Indian Inspired Lentils

Serves 6-8 Veg, V, Egg Free, Corn Free

- 1 Large yellow or brown onion, chopped, about 2½ cups
- 1½ Tbsp olive oil
- 1 cup chopped green bell pepper
- 3-4 cloves garlic, chopped
- 4 cups water
- 2 cups dried lentils
- 1 cup canned garbanzo beans, drained, or dried, prepared
- ¾ tsp ground ginger
- ¾ tsp ground coriander
- 2¾ tsp sea salt
- ½ tsp cumin
- ⅔ cup golden raisins

Serve as an exotic side dish or as a vegetarian/vegan entree. Chill and serve over salad greens as an Indian-inspired salad.

In a 4-qt pot, cook the onion in olive oil 5 minutes on medium heat, stirring occasionally. Add the bell pepper and garlic, and cook 4 minutes. Add the water, cover and bring to a boil. Stir in lentils and return to a boil. Reduce heat to low and simmer uncovered 25-30 minutes until lentils are tender and water is absorbed. While the lentils cook, stir in the garbanzo beans, ginger, coriander, salt and cumin. Add raisins the last 5-10 minutes of cooking time.

Quinoa with Herbs & Olives

Makes 3-4 Entree Salads or 8 Sides Veg, V, Egg Free, Corn Free

- 1 cup finely chopped yellow onion
- 2 Tbsp olive oil
- 2 cloves garlic, minced
- 1½ cups quinoa, well rinsed
- 2¼ cups water
- 1½ tsp sea salt
- ⅓ cup chopped fresh Italian flat leaf parsley
- ⅓ cup chopped fresh basil
- ⅓ cup chopped fresh dill
- ¼ cup sliced black olives
- ¼ cup sliced green olives
- ¼ cup sliced kalamata olives
- ½ cup toasted chopped walnuts
- ½ cup toasted pine nuts

Hot or cold, this winning blend of herbs, olives and nuts is as wholesome and nutritious as it is delicious.

In a 3-qt saucepan, cook the onion in the oil on medium heat 3 minutes, stirring occasionally. Stir in the garlic and cook 1 minute. Add the quinoa and cook while stirring 1 minute. Stir in the water and salt, and bring to a boil. Lower heat, cover and simmer 15 minutes, until water is absorbed. Remove from heat and let stand 5 minutes. Add herbs, olives, walnuts and pine nuts. Toss to combine. Serve hot as a side with chicken or fish or chill to serve as a salad.

Asparagus with Creamy Garlic Sauce

Serves 4-6

Veg, V, Egg Free, Corn Free

- ½ lb cauliflower (½ of 1 small head), cut into chunks, excluding stem
- 2 cups water
- ¼ cup + 2 Tbsp **light** coconut milk
- ⅓ tsp garlic powder
- ⅓ tsp sea salt, to taste
- 1½ lb fresh asparagus

Lovely enough for the fanciest dinner party, this dish is pure, clean nutrition for even the most health-conscious of eaters. Quick and simple to make and easy to double.

In a 2-qt pot, cook the cauliflower in the water 10 minutes, covered, until very soft. Remove from heat. Drain well. Into a blender, put cauliflower, milk, garlic powder and salt and blend until smooth. If sauce seems too thick, add 1-2 Tbsp of water and blend again. Snap asparagus spears at the base to remove any tough, unwanted portion. Steam, saute or grill the asparagus until tender-crisp. Drain well and arrange on a platter. Pour some Creamy Garlic Sauce over asparagus and serve remaining sauce in a small pitcher or sauce boat at the table.

Orange Cranberry Sauce

Makes about 5 Cups

Veg, V, Egg Free, Corn Free

- 6 cups fresh cranberries, washed and sorted
- 1 cup freshly grated orange zest
- ½ cup fresh-squeezed orange juice
- 1¼ cups coconut palm sugar
- 1 tsp liquid stevia

Tangy and sweet, with an infusion of fresh orange. Why buy an overpriced, processed product full of refined white sugar when you can quickly whip this up in advance?

In a 3-qt saucepan, bring all ingredients, except for sugar and stevia, to a boil. Lower heat, stir and cook about 10 minutes until most of the cranberries have popped. Remove from heat and stir in sugar and stevia. Enjoy hot, at room temperature, or chill before serving.

Garlic Mashed Cauli

Makes about 3 Cups or 4-5 Servings

Veg, V, Egg Free, Corn Free

- 2 lb cauliflower (1 very large head), 7-8 cups chopped
- 1 Tbsp plain rice or almond milk
- 1¾ tsp sea salt
- 1¼-1½ tsp garlic powder
- ½ tsp ghee, optional
- ½ cup white beans such as cannellini or navy beans, rinsed well using a strainer and drained on a paper towel

My version of low-glycemic mashed potatoes. They taste like you're cheating and getting away with something decadent. For extra creamy, use coconut milk.

In a 4-qt pot, cook the cauliflower in 5 cups of water, covered, about 10 minutes, until very soft. Drain well using a colander. Into a blender, put the cauliflower with the milk, salt, garlic powder and ghee, if using. Blend on low speed 15 seconds. Scrape sides of blender, push cauliflower down and blend on low again. Repeat as needed. Once cauliflower is coarsely ground, add beans and blend on low speed just until smooth, but not creamed.

Creamy Brown Rice Risotto with Mushrooms

Serves 6-8 Veg, V, Egg Free, Corn Free

- 1 lb cauliflower (1 medium head) or 5-6 cups cut up
- 4 cups water
- ⅔ cup **light** coconut milk
- 2 cloves garlic equalling 2-3 tsp, chopped
- 1¾-2 tsp sea salt, to taste
- 2 Tbsp dry white wine
- 2 Tbsp olive oil
- ¾ lb crimini mushrooms, sliced
- ⅔ cup shallots or brown onion, chopped
- 2 Tbsp fresh rosemary, optional
- 3½ cups cooked brown rice

In a 4-qt pot, cook the cauliflower in the water 10 minutes, covered, until very soft. Remove from heat and drain. Into a blender, pour the coconut milk and ½ of the cauliflower. Blend 20-30 seconds. Add remaining cauliflower and garlic, and blend again. Add the salt and wine, and blend until smooth. Set aside.

In a large skillet, cook the mushrooms and shallots (and rosemary, if desired) in the olive oil on medium heat 10 minutes until soft. Stir in the cauliflower sauce. Once mixture is blended and heated, add the rice. Stir until mixed and heated through. Do not over-mix, which will make the rice mushy. Serve immediately or, if serving later, spoon into a covered baking dish to reheat at 350° 20 minutes or until heated through.

Savor the hints of wine and rosemary. Who would guess that the creaminess of this risotto is basically cauliflower? So, "dress up" a simple dinner of grilled chicken or fish by slipping in this highly nutritious vegetable. To save time, make a big batch of brown rice. I use a rice cooker which is wonderful! Divide and freeze the rice in 1-qt zip bags that are flattened so that they're thin and stack well in the freezer. When you make a recipe that calls for cooked brown rice, simply pull a bag out of the freezer. Very convenient!

Molasses Stuffed Acorn Squash

Serves 4 Veg, V, Egg Free, Corn Free

- 2 acorn or butternut squash, halved, seeds removed
- ½ cup water
- 1 Tbsp grapeseed, sesame, walnut or avocado oil*
- • sea salt
- • cinnamon
- 2-2½ cups Nutty Molasses Granola, p.81
- 3-3½ Tbsp coconut nectar

*Note: These oils are ideal to use at high temperatures and also lend great flavor.

Stuffed Acorn Squash says "autumn" and "harvest time." Perfect with poultry. Extra festive with Cornish game hens!

Preheat oven to 350°. Into a baking dish sized to fit the halved squashes, pour the ½ cup of water. Brush each cut side of squash with grapeseed oil or one of the other oils suggested. Sprinkle each with sea salt and cinnamon, and place them, cut side up, in the baking dish. Bake uncovered 25 minutes. Remove from oven.

In a small bowl, mix the Nutty Molasses Granola with the coconut nectar. Spoon some of the mixture into the seed cavity of each halved squash. Return to oven and bake another 5-10 minutes, or until squash is tender when pierced with a fork.

Orange Pecan Brown Rice

Serves 6 Veg, V, Egg Free, Corn Free

- 1 large orange, grated, then squeezed
- ¾ cup yellow or brown onion, minced
- ¾ cup celery, chopped
- 2 Tbsp grapeseed oil
- 1¼ tsp sea salt
- ¼ tsp dried thyme
- 2½ Tbsp coconut nectar
- 1⅔ cup water
- 1 cup uncooked long grain brown rice
- ⅔ cup chopped pecans

An excellent accompaniment to poultry. We love it with Cornish game hens and Molasses Stuffed Acorn Squash . It's also wonderful with the Chicken de Provence, p.33, or the Salmon with Creamy Pesto & Walnuts on p.27.

Grate the orange and measure ⅓ cup of the grated zest. From the orange, squeeze ⅓ cup of juice. Add it to the zest and set aside. In a 3-4 qt saucepan, cook the onion and celery in the oil on medium heat about 5 minutes. Remove from heat. Stir in the grated zest, orange juice, salt, thyme, coconut nectar and water, and bring to a boil. Add the rice. When it returns to a boil, lower the heat and simmer covered for 50 minutes. Stir in the pecans and serve.

Herbed Turkey Dressing

Serves 8-10 Veg, V & Egg Free (w/ vegetable broth & egg replacer), Corn Free

- 2¼ cups chopped yellow or brown onion
- 3½ cups sliced celery, about 6 stalks
- ¼ cup olive oil
- 2 large eggs
- 1¼ cups chicken stock or broth
- 1½ tsp coriander
- 1 Tbsp fresh sage or ½ tsp ground
- 1 Tbsp fresh thyme or ½ tsp dried
- 2 Tbsp fresh parsley
- ½ tsp Herbs de Provence, optional
- 2½ tsp sea salt
- ½ tsp black pepper
- 10 cups cubed GF brown rice bread such as Glutino® or Ener-G® brands
- 1 cup chopped pecans, optional

What a joy! Now on Thanksgiving or any other day when they pass the dressing, you no longer need to say "no thanks." On top of that, your family will love this dressing without even knowing it's GF.

In a skillet, sauté the onion and celery in the oil over medium-high heat covered, stirring occasionally, until soft. Preheat oven to 375°. Spray a 2½-qt baking dish with grapeseed oil. In a large bowl, whisk the eggs. Whisk in the chicken stock, herbs, spices, salt and pepper. Add onion and celery, including the oil. Stir in bread and pecans, if using, and mix thoroughly until bread has absorbed the liquid. Turn into baking dish, cover and bake 35 minutes.

Glazed Yams with Cranberries

Serves 12 Veg, V, Egg Free, Corn Free

- 4 lb yams, peeled and cut into 1 by 1½" chunks
- 3 Tbsp olive oil
- 1 tsp garlic powder
- ¾ tsp sea salt, divided: ¼ tsp and ½ tsp
- 2 cups fresh cranberries, washed and sorted
- 1½ Tbsp coconut nectar
- ¼ tsp liquid stevia
- 2 Tbsp fresh orange juice
- 3 Tbsp fresh grated orange zest

Colorful and nutritious, this Delightful dish has only 300 calories and about 3½g fat, but about 7g fiber, 2½g protein and 1¼g potassium. It's also high in vitamins C and B-6, and the mineral manganese. Want a zesty change for a salad? Leftovers are great over shredded cabbage with Sweet & Tangy Asian Dressing p.99.

Preheat oven to 375°. Spray a large, high-rimmed baking sheet and a 2-qt baking dish with grapeseed oil. In a large bowl, toss and coat yams with the olive oil, garlic powder and ¼ tsp salt. Spread yams evenly on the baking sheet and roast 15 minutes until **slightly** soft. Turn yams back into the bowl and set aside. In a 2-qt saucepan, cook cranberries on medium-high heat 5 minutes, stirring occasionally. Remove from heat and stir in coconut nectar and stevia. Add cranberries to the bowl of yams with orange juice, orange zest and ½ tsp salt. Toss gently to mix without making yams mushy. Turn into the baking dish. Bake covered 25-30 minutes, just until heated through.

Snacks & Treats

Layered Herbs & Cream

Makes 8 Pie Slices or 12 Squares   Veg, V, Egg Free, Corn Free

- ½ cup **whole** coconut milk
- 2 Tbsp water
- 1 14 oz can garbanzo beans, rinsed and drained on a paper towel
- 1 tsp sea salt
- 1 medium clove garlic, chopped
- 6 nine inch brown rice tortillas
- • olive oil, preferably applied using an oil mister (see note on p.127)

Green Onion and Olive Filling

- 3 Tbsp from the white, lighter sections of green onions, thinly sliced
- 4 Tbsp from the green tops of green onions, thinly sliced
- ½ cup of your favorite olives, finely chopped

Dill and Walnut Filling

- 3 Tbsp fresh dill, snipped or chopped finely
- 3 Tbsp yellow or brown onion, minced finely
- ½ cup finely chopped walnuts

Basil and Sundried Tomato Pesto Filling

- ¼ cup fresh basil, finely chopped
- 2 Tbsp finely chopped sundried tomatoes
- ½ cup pine nuts or walnuts, finely chopped

This recipe makes a smashing tray of hors d'oeuvres for a party, or an alluring accompaniment for Cream of Broc & Cauli Soup, or Creamy Carrot Soup. As pretty as they look, they are packed with protein, fiber and nutrients.

In a blender or food processor, blend the milk, water, garbanzo beans, salt and garlic until smooth. Use a silicone spatula to remove the garbanzo bean filling to a medium bowl. Select and stir in the other filling ingredients of your choice.

Preheat oven to 350°. Brush or spray a baking sheet with grapeseed oil. Working with 1 tortilla at a time on the baking sheet, lightly spray or brush both sides of the tortilla with a small amount of olive oil. Use a brush to spread oil evenly. Bake each tortilla for 1½ minutes exactly. If overcooked, tortilla will quickly become too crisp. Remove the tortilla to a flat platter or cutting board. Spread about ⅓ cup of the filling evenly over it. Repeat the process, stacking each new tortilla on top of the previous one. When you've used all of your filing, place your final "cap" tortilla on top. With the palm of your hand, very gently press the top surface of your stacked tortillas down to even the filling and make the top flat. Immediately cover with a very damp paper towel and then a square of wax paper followed by saran wrap. Be sure it is tightly covered to keep the moisture in. Refrigerate overnight or for at least 8 hours.

To serve as a snack, cut the stacked tortillas like a pie. If using as hors d'oeuvres, cut into a grid, making 1½" squares, triangles or diamond shapes. Keep covered and refrigerated until serving.

Lentil Walnut Tapenade

Makes about 5 Cups   Veg, V, Egg Free, Corn Free

- 2 cups water
- 1 cup dried green lentils
- 2 cups toasted walnuts
- ⅔ cup olive oil
- ⅓ cup + 1 Tbsp lemon juice
- 6 cloves garlic, minced, preferably with a garlic press
- 1 15 oz can black olives, sliced, about 1½ cups
- 2 tsp sea salt

I could eat this on almost anything! A great appetizer for a party with Baked Corn-Free Tortilla Chips, p.123, or GF crackers, and sensational as a salad topper.

In a 2-qt saucepan, bring the water to a boil. Add the lentils and return to a boil. Reduce heat to medium and cook only 5 minutes. Drain using a wire strainer and run cold water over the lentils to prevent them from cooking further. Drain well. Into a blender, put 1 cup of the toasted walnuts at a time and pulse 2-3 times until walnuts are coarsely chopped. Remove to a bowl. Next, put ½ of the lentils into blender and pulse 5-6 times. Scrape down sides and stir when needed. Pulse again until lentils are crumbly. Remove to bowl with the walnuts and repeat with remaining lentils. Stir all remaining ingredients into bowl. If tapenade seems dry, add 1-2 Tbsp more lemon juice.

Spicy Walnut Red Pepper Dip

Makes 1⅓ Cups   Veg, V, Egg Free, Corn Free

- ¾ lb fresh Roma tomatoes, chopped and drained, or 1 14-15 oz can crushed or diced tomatoes, drained
- ½ Tbsp olive oil
- 2 cloves garlic, minced
- ¼ tsp cayenne pepper, or more for extra heat
- ½ tsp sea salt
- ⅛ tsp black pepper
- 1½ cups walnuts
- ¼ cup almond meal

Quick and simple to make. A nutritious, protein-packed snack or fabulous hors d'oeuvre.

Into a blender or food processor, pour ¼ cup of the tomatoes, oil, garlic, cayenne pepper, salt and black pepper. Blend 30 seconds. Add the walnuts and chop on low speed until crumbly. Add remaining tomatoes and blend on low just 5-10 seconds so that tomatoes are reduced but not pureed. Stir in almond meal and serve.

Baked Corn-Free Tortilla Chips

Makes 75-150 Chips — Veg, V, Egg Free, Corn Free

3-6 brown rice tortillas
- olive oil, preferably applied using an oil mister
- sea salt

Preheat oven to 350°. Brush or spray a baking sheet with olive oil. On the baking sheet, **lightly** spray and then brush both sides of each tortilla. Sprinkle both sides very lightly with salt. With a sharp knife or kitchen scissors, cut the tortillas into 1-2" strips. I cut the tortillas 3 at a time with kitchen scissors. Next cut the strips in 1½-2" lengths.

Spread tortilla strips on the baking sheet without overlapping. Bake 8-9 minutes. Remove strips that have turned a golden color to a bowl. Return the baking sheet with the remaining tortilla strips to the oven 1-2 minutes more, checking to remove them as they turn golden. Cool the chips on the sheet or in a bowl, and serve. Store leftover chips in a zip bag. They should keep for 7-10 days, or even longer.

Because corn is a food that causes inflammation, it's wonderful to have a healthy, delicious alternative which is still gluten free. For people who have inflammatory issues, it's so much fun to be able to munch away without a care! To best prepare these chips, I recommend using a mister, such as a Misto® or other similar type of sprayer. A mister allows you to spread the oil much more sparingly than when applying with a brush. After spraying it on, spread using a brush for best results.

Hummus

Makes 4½ Cups — Veg, V, Egg Free, Corn Free

- 2 15 oz cans garbanzo beans, rinsed and drained well
- 4-6 cloves garlic or 2½ tsp garlic powder
- 1½ tsp sea salt
- ¾ cup + 2 Tbsp tahini
- ¾ cup lemon juice
- ⅓-½ cup water
- 2 Tbsp olive oil
- ¼ tsp cumin
- ¼ tsp cayenne pepper

So simple to make, and so good, it's gobbled up faster than you can say "chickpea." We like to blend in other ingredients such as olives, sundried tomatoes or peperoncini to create other hummus varieties.

Blend all ingredients, except toppings, in a food processor or blender. If mixture seems too thick, stir in a Tbsp or more of water or lemon juice. Blend on high for 30 seconds for a creamy smooth texture. Place in serving bowl. Make a small well in center of hummus and fill with olive oil. Garnish with your choice of toppings.

Optional Toppings

Chopped cilantro or parsley, chopped tomatoes, toasted sesame seeds, toasted pine nuts, sprinkled paprika, pepper or Za'atar (a Lebanese herb blend).

Café Nuts

Makes 3 Cups — Veg, V, Egg Free, Corn Free

- 3 cups any combination raw nuts such as almonds, walnuts, cashews, hazelnuts...
- 1 Tbsp grapeseed oil
- 2 Tbsp coconut nectar
- ⅛ tsp liquid stevia, to taste
- ½ tsp cayenne pepper, or more if you like it hot!
- 1 tsp sea salt
- 2½ Tbsp fresh rosemary leaves, chopped or snipped

Preheat oven to 350°. Brush a jelly roll pan or cookie sheet generously with grapeseed oil. In a bowl, combine the nuts with oil, coconut nectar and stevia, tossing to cover thoroughly. Add the pepper, salt and rosemary. Stir until the nuts are completely coated. Spread evenly on the prepared baking sheet and toast in the oven about 8 minutes until light, golden brown. Cool completely on baking sheet. Use a spatula to loosen and remove nuts. Store in an air-tight container.

I love these nuts! Our neighbor gave them to us one year at Christmas time and I was crazy about the sweet/salty/hot/rosemary flavors with all that crunch. So I figured out how to reproduce them without butter or sugar. I hope you enjoy them as much as we do.

Crunchy Snack Mix

Makes 3¼ Cups — Veg, V, Egg Free, Corn Free (without popcorn)

- 1 Tbsp grapeseed oil
- 2½ Tbsp coconut nectar
- ⅛ tsp + 5 drops liquid stevia
- ⅓ tsp sea salt

Who would think of putting split peas and lentils into a sweet & crunchy snack mix?! But they add color and crunch, and a burst of nutrition. (Don't tell the kids!)

Mix 1

- ⅔ cup whole raw almonds
- 1 cup GF Whole O's cereal such as Nature's Path® brand
- ½ cup crispy brown rice cereal such as Barbara's® brand
- ¾ cup popped popcorn
- ⅓ cup mini chocolate chips*

Mix 2

- ⅔ cup slivered almonds
- ½ cup crispy brown rice cereal such as Barbara's® brand
- ⅓ cup red lentils, soaked 20 minutes, drained until dry
- ⅓ cup split peas, soaked 1 hour, drained until dry
- ⅓ cup naturally sweetened, dried cranberries

Preheat oven to 350°. Brush or spray a jelly roll pan or cookie sheet generously with grapeseed oil. In a medium bowl, combine the oil, coconut nectar, stevia and salt. Add remaining ingredients for the mix of your choice and toss to cover thoroughly. Spread the mixture on prepared baking sheet and toast in the oven about 8 minutes until light golden. Cool completely on baking sheet. Use a spatula to loosen and remove. Store in an air-tight container.

*See suggested chocolates in Stocking you GF, DF, SF Pantry, p.7.

Fruit Smoothies

Serves 2 Veg, V, Egg Free, Corn Free

- 1¼ cups chilled vanilla rice or almond milk
- 2 cups frozen strawberries (about 12)
- 1 cup frozen blueberries*
- 1 medium banana, frozen overnight
- 8 drops liquid stevia, optional

A refreshing treat! Try substituting blueberries with raspberries or blackberries. Freeze the unpeeled banana overnight. Keeping the peel on will prevent browning.

*Note: If using frozen raspberries or blackberries, instead of blueberries, use ½ cup and 8-10 drops of stevia, if desired.

Pour milk into blender and add ½ of the strawberries and ½ of the blueberries. Blend on "crush ice" mode until fruit is broken up. Halve banana to remove peel and add it, with remaining strawberries and blueberries, and blend again on "crush ice" mode until fruit is broken up. Blend on "chop" mode 5-10 seconds, then "mix" mode for 5 seconds. Add the stevia, if using, and blend on "puree" mode for 5-10 seconds.

Ice Cream Cones

Makes 1 Cone Veg, V, Egg Free, Corn Free

- 1 brown rice tortilla for each ice cream cone desired
- • olive oil, preferably in an oil mister*
- • a small amount of coconut nectar
- • cinnamon

*Note: To best prepare these cones, I recommend using a mister, such as a Misto® or similar type of sprayer. Using a mister allows you to spread the oil much more sparingly than when applying it with a brush. After spraying oil on, spread it using a brush for best results.

Preheat oven to 350°. Brush or spray a baking sheet with grapeseed oil. I recommend making only 2 cones at a time. On the prepared baking sheet, spray and then brush both sides of each tortilla with a very small amount of oil. Drizzle both sides with a very small amount of coconut nectar, about ⅛ tsp for each side. Lightly sprinkle both sides of tortillas with cinnamon, then brush again thoroughly. Lay the tortillas on the baking sheet without overlapping. Bake only 3 minutes, to soften tortillas. Remove from oven and immediately wrap each tortilla into a cone shape. To create a conical shape, use oven-safe objects such as an unshelled walnut to support the small end and the metal beaters from a mixer or a Pyrex type measuring cup for the larger end. Set the cones down on the side with the overlapping edges or seam. Bake 9 minutes. Remove from oven and carefully remove the "shaping objects" (beaters, measuring cups and walnuts). Do this gently without breaking the cones as they begin to become crispy. Roll the cones over so the seam side is up and return to oven. Bake another 3 minutes or until golden. Fill cones with DF ice cream of your choice and enjoy, or store in an airtight container for use later. The cones should keep for 1-2 weeks.

What a treat! How wonderful it is to be able to offer the GF child in your life a sweet, crispy ice cream cone. Even better, enjoy them together!

Cookies & Bars

Chocolate Chip Cookies

Makes 22 Cookies Veg, V & Egg Free (w/ egg replacer) Corn Free

- 3 large eggs
- ½ cup + 1½ Tbsp grapeseed oil
- 1¼ cup coconut palm sugar
- ¾ tsp liquid stevia
- 1½ tsp vanilla
- 1 tsp sea salt
- 1½ tsp aluminum-free, GF baking powder
- 1½ tsp baking soda
- ½ tsp xanthan gum
- 2½ cups almond meal
- 1 cup + 2 Tbsp brown rice flour
- 1 Tbsp tapioca flour
- ½-⅔ cup DF dark chocolate chips (see suggested chocolates on p.7)
- ¾ cup chopped walnuts, optional

So chewy and delicious, but with none of the white sugar, white flour, butter or shortening found in traditional cookies. Instead, these chocolate chip cookies are made predominantly from ground almonds and ground brown rice. They have about 11.7g unrefined, natural sugar, but, unlike other cookies, each of these GF, DF and nauturally sweetened cookies provides 5g protein and 2g fiber.

Preheat oven to 325°. Spray a baking sheet with grapeseed oil. In a large bowl, whisk eggs, oil, sugar, stevia and vanilla together until smooth. Add salt, baking powder, baking soda and xanthan gum, and whisk until sugar is dissolved and consistency is smooth. With a wooden spoon, stir in almond meal and both flours. Add chocolate and, if desired, walnuts. Form 2" mounds of dough on baking sheet. Dough will be sticky. Bake 12 minutes. Cool on baking sheet 4 minutes before removing with a spatula.

Shortbread

Makes 16 Cookies Veg, Egg Free, Corn Free

- 1¼ cups brown rice flour
- ½ cup arrowroot flour
- ½ tsp + a pinch sea salt
- ¼ tsp cinnamon
- ¼ tsp baking soda
- ½ tsp xanthan gum
- ⅓ cup coconut oil, softened
- 2 tsp ghee, melted
- 3½ Tbsp coconut nectar
- ½ tsp liquid stevia

Enjoy this healthy version of shortbread. It tastes so much like other recipes you've tried, but with much less and only natural sugar. A friend said, "but I can taste the butter. I can't believe you didn't use any!"

Preheat oven to 300°. Spray an 8x8 pan with grapeseed oil. In a bowl, whisk the 2 flours, salt, cinnamon, baking soda and xanthan gum. Add coconut oil and ghee, and mix well using the back of a spoon to press and stir. Add the coconut nectar and stevia, and mix thoroughly. Press into pan with the back of the spoon to flatten, making the surface even and smooth. Use the tip of a fork to press dots evenly across the top. Bake 30-35 minutes. Remove from oven and cut into squares immediately, then cool completely in the pan.

Dark Chocolate-Chunk Cookies

Makes 24 Cookies   Veg, V & Egg Free (w/ egg replacer), Corn Free

- 1 cup grapeseed oil
- 1 cup coconut palm sugar
- 2 large eggs
- 1 tsp vanilla
- 1 tsp liquid stevia
- 1¼ tsp sea salt
- 1 tsp baking soda
- 1 tsp aluminum-free, GF baking powder
- ½ cup + 2 Tbsp unsweetened cocoa powder
- ½ tsp xanthan gum
- 1½ cups brown rice flour
- 1¼ cups almond meal
- ½ cup dark chocolate chips or chunks*
- ½ cup chopped walnuts, optional

Have a double dose of dark chocolate in these chewy, rich delights. They taste like you've really gone off the deep end on a splurge, but the truth is that dark chocolate is high in heart-healthy nutrients and anti-oxidants. All that sweetness comes only from natural, unrefined sweeteners. On top of that, almond meal helps regulate blood sugar, and contributes protein and fiber.

Preheat oven to 350°. In a mixing bowl, whisk the oil and sugar. Add the eggs, vanilla, stevia, salt, baking soda, baking powder, cocoa powder and xanthan gum. Whisk until sugar has dissolved and consistency is smooth. Stir in the flour and almond meal with a wooden spoon. Dough will be oily. Stir in the chocolate pieces and walnuts, if desired. Make 1½" mounds on an ungreased baking sheet 1" apart. Bake 9-10 minutes. Don't over-bake. Cool 3 minutes before removing with a spatula.

Coconut Macaroons (PHOTO P.128)

Makes 10-12 Cookies   Veg, Corn Free

- 3 cups unsweetened medium-flake coconut**
- ½ cup coconut nectar
- ½ tsp liquid stevia
- ¼ tsp + ⅛ tsp sea salt
- ⅔ cup (about 4 extra large) egg whites, whisked
- 1 tsp vanilla
- 2 Tbsp coconut flour
- ½ tsp xanthan gum
- ⅓ cup chocolate chips* optional, for chocolate dipped

Coconut is a wonderful, healthy food. See my blog (www.delightfullyfree.com) for info on nutritional advantages of coconut flour, sugar, oil and meat. Get your "dose" of coconut by enjoying a cookie or two.

Preheat oven to 325°. Spray a baking sheet with grapeseed oil. In a medium bowl, mix the coconut, coconut nectar, stevia and salt. Stir in egg whites and vanilla. Add flour and xanthan gum, and mix well. Allow 5 minutes for mixture to thicken. Gently squeeze together 2" mounds on baking sheet and bake 18-20 minutes. Cookies will be golden and will firm up more as they cool. For chocolate dipped macaroons, melt the chocolate chips in a double boiler over simmering water. Dip the top of each cookie and allow chocolate to harden either at room temperature or more quickly in the refrigerator.

* See suggested chocolates in "Stocking your GF, DF, SF Pantry," p.7.

** If you cannot find medium-flake coconut that is unsweetened, use Bob's Red Mill® or Let's Do Organic® brand which are unsweetened and come in a larger flake. Chop it easily and quickly in a food processor or food chopper to a medium-size flake.

Chocolate Ambrosia Cookies

Makes about 24 Cookies Veg, V, Egg Free, Corn Free

- ¾ cup grapeseed oil
- ¾ cup coconut palm sugar
- ⅓ cup + 1 Tbsp coconut nectar
- 1 tsp liquid stevia
- 3 Tbsp water
- 1¼ tsp sea salt
- ½ tsp baking soda
- 2 cups almond meal
- ½ cup brown rice flour
- 2 Tbsp arrowroot flour
- 1½ tsp xanthan gum
- 1⅓ cup uncooked creamy buckwheat cereal, like Bob's Red Mill® or Pocono®
- ⅔ cup coarsely chopped, slivered blanched almonds
- 1 cup unsweetened medium or large flake coconut, such as Bob's Red Mill® or Let's Do Organic®
- ⅔ cup unsweetened, unsulfured dried cherries, such as Trader Joe's®
- ½ cup DF, dark chocolate chips or chopped DF dark chocolate (see suggested chocolates on p.7)

Sometimes you just want more than chocolate chips in your cookie...try these.

Preheat oven to 350°. Lightly spray a baking sheet with grapeseed oil. In a large bowl, whisk together oil, sugar, coconut nectar, stevia, water, salt and baking soda until smooth. With a sturdy spoon, stir in almond meal, both flours, xanthan gum and buckwheat, and mix well. Stir in last 4 ingredients. Dough will be stiff. Form 2" mounds of dough and press down slightly with fingers on baking sheet. Bake 11-12 minutes until golden. Cool completely before removing.

This scrumptious cookie is bursting with an assortment of flavors and textures! Almonds, the main ingredient, are rich in protein and fiber, and help decrease spikes in blood sugar. The other major ingredient, buckwheat, which is very nutritious, lends a nutty crunch and also helps to keep blood sugar levels in check.

Faux Peanut Butter Cookies

Makes 18 Cookies Veg, V & Egg Free (w/ egg replacer), Corn Free

- ½ cup grapeseed oil
- ½ cup sunflower seed butter
- 1 cup coconut palm sugar
- 1 tsp vanilla
- 1 large egg, whisked
- ¾ tsp sea salt
- 1 tsp baking soda
- ½ cup almond meal
- ½ cup brown rice flour
- ¼ cup + 2 Tbsp coconut flour
- ¼ cup chopped, toasted almonds for extra crunch, optional

Peanuts are high on the list of inflammatory foods. For those who have inflammatory issues, it's heaven to gobble up these chewy, crunchy, peanutty cookies right out of the oven. You would never know there's no trace of peanut in them.

Preheat oven to 350°. In a bowl, whisk oil, sunflower seed butter, sugar and vanilla together. Rest batter a few minutes until coconut sugar has dissolved. Stir in remaining ingredients. Drop tablespoonfuls onto an ungreased baking sheet, then press down gently with fingers to form a round, slightly thick shape. Press a fork into cookies just enough to make the traditional crosshatch pattern. Dip fork in brown rice flour occasionally to keep it from getting too sticky. Bake 7 minutes for chewy cookies and 9 minutes for crunchy ones.

Black Bean Brownies

Makes 24 Brownies   Veg, V and Egg Free (w/ egg replacer), Corn Free

- 2 large eggs
- 1 Tbsp water
- ⅓ cup grapeseed oil
- 1½ tsp vanilla
- ¾ tsp liquid stevia
- 1 15 oz can black beans, rinsed well using a wire strainer and drained on a paper towel
- 1¼ cup coconut palm sugar
- 2 Tbsp coconut nectar
- ¾ cup unsweetened cocoa powder
- ¼ tsp sea salt
- 1½ tsp aluminum-free, GF baking powder
- 1 tsp baking soda
- ¾ tsp xanthan gum
- ½ cup chopped almonds or walnuts, optional
- ½ cup dark chocolate chips or chunks, optional*

What if I were to tell you that every one of these brownies has about 2.8g protein, 2g fiber, with only about 7.4g fat and 11g natural sugar? According to the California Apple Association, even medium-size apples contain about 16g natural sugar. Because they contain no refined sugar, these brownies, like an apple, are a beneficial food with only about 142 calories each. And did I mention that the main ingredient is black beans? Well, I'm Delighted to say it's true. And it's so easy! Everything goes in a blender!

Preheat oven to 350°. Brush or spray a 9x13 pan with grapeseed oil. In a blender or food processor,** blend the eggs, water, oil, vanilla and stevia 10 seconds, then add the beans and blend 30 seconds. Scrape sides of the blender with a silicone spatula as needed. Next, add all remaining ingredients except for the chocolate chips or chunks, and the nuts. Process 1-2 minutes until all is thoroughly blended. Stir in the chocolate chips or chunks, and nuts, if desired. Pour the batter into the pan. Sprinkle with additional nuts, if desired, and bake 22 minutes, or until a toothpick comes out clean. Cool on a wire rack.

* See suggested chocolates in "Stocking your GF, DF, SF Pantry," p.7.

** If you have an immersion blender, it works very well with this recipe, mixing everything in a large bowl instead of in a blender. Use the blending wand for the first 6 ingredients, and then the whisk attachment or a hand mixer for the remainder.

Oatmeal Cookies

Makes about 32 Cookies Veg, V, Egg Free, Corn Free

- ⅔ cup organic all vegetable shortening such as Spectrum® brand
- 1¾ cups coconut palm sugar
- ½ tsp liquid stevia
- 2½ cups brown rice flour
- ¾ tsp sea salt
- 1 tsp baking soda
- 1½ tsp aluminum-free, GF baking powder
- 2½ tsp cinnamon
- 1/16 tsp nutmeg
- 1½ tsp xanthan gum
- 1¾ cups soaked, **unbaked** steel cut oats (see p.11)
- 1 jumbo 2½ gallon plastic zip bag
- ⅔ cup raisins, optional

Preheat oven to 350°. Brush or spray a baking sheet with grapeseed oil. In a small bowl, cream the shortening, sugar and stevia. In a large bowl, whisk the flour, salt, baking soda, baking powder, cinnamon, nutmeg and xanthan gum. Mix the oats into the large bowl. Stir in the shortening-sugar mixture using the back of a spoon until the color and texture have evened out. The dough will be very dry. Pour the dough into the plastic bag, squeeze the air out and seal it. Roll the dough with a rolling pin, moving the dough around inside the bag until it has all become moist and holds together. Dump back into the bowl, add the raisins, if desired, and make 1½" balls spaced 2" apart. Press down slightly with fingers. Bake 13 minutes, or until tops of cookies feel slightly firm. Cool completely before removing with a spatula.

Because this book prioritizes nutrition as well as delicious food, I chose not to use rolled oats in my recipes. Rolled oats get their flat, flaky texture from the processing they undergo. This changes them into a high-glycemic food that quickly elevates insulin and blood sugar levels. This, in turn, stimulates fat storage, increases hyperactivity, compromises attention span, and even reduces performance in sports and physical activities. Steel cut oats, on the other hand, are a whole oat which contain all of the fiber and density of a natural oat. This means that they cause the proper, slower release of glucose into the blood stream as a nutritious food.

Cranberry Date Bars (PHOTO P.128)

Makes 24 Bars — Veg, V, Egg Free, Corn Free

- ½ cup + 3 Tbsp grapeseed oil
- 1 cup coconut palm sugar
- ¼ cup water
- 1¼ tsp liquid stevia
- 1¼ tsp sea salt
- ½ tsp baking soda
- 1 tsp xanthan gum
- 2 cups almond meal
- ½ cup brown rice flour
- ¼ cup arrowroot flour
- 1½ cups creamy buckwheat cereal such as Bob's Red Mill® or Pocono®
- 1 cup chopped walnuts

Filling

- 8 oz chopped dates, about 2 cups
- 12 oz fresh or frozen cranberries, about 3¼ cups, washed and sorted
- 2 Tbsp coconut palm sugar
- 15 drops liquid stevia

Perfect as a nutritious, pick-me-up snack, yet also sophisticated and delicious enough for a ladies' tea.

In a 2½-qt saucepan, stir the dates and cranberries on medium-low heat 10 minutes or until cranberries have popped. Cover when not stirring. Remove from heat, stir in the 2 Tbsp sugar, stevia and set aside. Preheat oven to 350°. Spray a 9x13 baking dish with grapeseed oil. In a large bowl, stir together the oil, sugar, water, stevia, salt, baking soda and xanthan gum. Add remaining cookie ingredients and mix with a wooden spoon. Lightly press about ⅔ into the pan using a square of wax paper. Bake 10 minutes. Spread filling over the base, scatter remaining cookie mixture over the top and press down lightly. Bake 12 minutes. Cool completely and cut into bars.

Raisin Squares (PHOTO P.128)

Makes about 24 Squares — Veg, V, Egg Free, Corn Free

- ⅔ cup grapeseed oil
- 1¼ cups coconut palm sugar
- 1 tsp liquid stevia
- 1⅔ cups brown rice flour
- 1½ tsp sea salt
- ½ tsp baking soda
- 1½ tsp cinnamon
- 2 tsp xanthan gum
- 1½ cups soaked, **unbaked** steel cut oats (see p.11)

Filling

- ⅔ cup water
- 2 Tbsp tapioca flour
- 2 Tbsp lemon juice
- ⅓ cup coconut palm sugar
- ¾ tsp liquid stevia
- 2½ cups raisins

When I was a child, my friend's mom would make these cookies. I thought they were the most delicious treats ever. So, I kept her recipe, re-worked it to be GF, DF and SF, and now we're enjoying Raisin Squares again. I hope they will become a favorite in your neighborhood.

Preheat oven to 350°. Spray a 9x13 pan with grapeseed oil. In a small bowl, mix the oil, sugar and stevia. In a large bowl, whisk together flour, salt, baking soda, cinnamon and xanthan gum. Stir in oats and oil-sugar mixture and combine thoroughly until texture is consistent, moist and crumbly. Press ⅔ of the mixture into the bottom of pan. In a 2½-qt saucepan, stir together first 5 filling ingredients. Add raisins and cook on medium heat, stirring until it thickens. Continue to stir and cook 1 minute more. Remove from heat. Spoon raisin mixture over cookie base. Scatter remaining oat mixture over the top. Bake 25 minutes. Cool completely on a rack before cutting squares.

Cakes, Pies & Crumbles

Classic Chocolate Cake

Makes One 9" Layer — Veg, V and Egg Free (w/ egg replacer), Corn Free

- 3 large eggs
- 1 15 oz can black beans, rinsed and drained well on a paper towel
- 3 Tbsp grapeseed oil
- ½ cup unsweetened cocoa powder
- 1½ tsp vanilla
- ⅛ tsp sea salt
- 1½ tsp aluminum-free, GF baking powder
- 1 tsp baking soda
- 1 cup coconut palm sugar
- ¾ tsp liquid stevia
- 1 Tbsp coconut flour
- 1 Tbsp tapioca flour

So easy...it's all done in a blender!

How many times have we had to ask our GF, DF or SF child to pass on the birthday cake? I hope my cake and frosting recipes will change all that for your family as it has for mine. Don't bother mentioning to party guests that your cake is GF, DF & refined SF--they won't believe it anyway.

Preheat oven to 350°. Brush or spray a 9" cake pan with grapeseed oil. Line the bottom of the pan with parchment paper* and lightly oil it too. In a blender, blend the eggs 10 seconds**. Add the black beans and blend 1 minute. Add the oil, cocoa powder, vanilla, salt, baking powder, baking soda, sugar and stevia. Using a silicone spatula, stir the powdery ingredients into the wet ingredients, and then blend 30 seconds. Scrape the sides of the blender as needed. Mix in the coconut and tapioca flours using the spatula, and blend 1 minute. Pour batter into the prepared cake pan. The silicone spatula is helpful in getting all of the batter out of the blender. Bake about 22 minutes, or until a toothpick inserted in the center comes out clean. The center of the cake will be firm and slightly springy to the touch. Cool on a rack 15 minutes. Run a knife around the edge to loosen before turning the cake out. Allow cake to cool completely on the rack before frosting.

For cupcakes, use paper liners and fill each to almost full, about ¼ inch from the top. Bake 19-20 minutes. This recipe will make 9 cupcakes.

*To use parchment paper, which can be purchased at most markets, place cake pan, bottom side down, on the parchment paper. With a pencil, trace around the pan. Cut out the round of parchment paper and lay it in the bottom of pan.

** If you have an immersion blender, it works very well with this recipe, mixing everything in a large bowl instead of in a blender. Use the blending wand for the first 6 ingredients, and then the whisk attachment or a hand mixer for the remainder.

This delicious cake packs a big surprise...as flavorful and rich as it is, it is also amazingly healthy! The secret is that the main ingredient is black beans, followed by eggs, which are both protein packed, whole foods. Note that in this cake, there are only 2 tablespoons of flour and that flour is, again, very healthy and nutritious. For a spectacularly tall cake like the one shown, bake 3 of these layers and stack them using one of my frostings as a filling between layers. I recommend mixing one layer at a time. It's quick and easy!

Chocolate Frosting

Frosts and Fills a 2 Layer Cake   Veg & V*, Egg Free, Corn Free

- 2 cups **whole** coconut milk, divided: ½ cup + 1½ cups (2 cans needed)
- 2¼ tsp unflavored gelatin
- ¾ cup organic all vegetable shortening, such as Spectrum® brand
- ½ cup unsweetened cocoa powder
- ⅓ cup raw honey
- ¾ tsp liquid stevia
- 1 tsp vanilla
- ¼ tsp + ⅛ tsp sea salt
- ½ tsp xanthan gum

In a small bowl, whisk together gelatin and ½ cup of milk. In a 2-qt saucepan, on medium heat, warm remaining milk almost to a boil. Remove from heat before boiling. Whisk in gelatin mixture and continue stirring until dissolved. Refrigerate 20 minutes in the pan to cool slightly, stirring occasionally. Put shortening into a blender and add about ⅓ cup of the milk-gelatin mixture. Blend 20 seconds. Continue adding ⅓ cup at a time, blending 20 seconds each time, until all has been added, scraping sides of blender occasionally. Add cocoa powder, honey, stevia, vanilla and salt, and blend on low 30 seconds. Scrape sides, add xanthan gum and blend 10 seconds on low, then 40 seconds on high. Scrape sides of blender and blend 20 seconds on high. Pour into a 4 cup container, cover and refrigerate 4-5 hours until firm. Frosted cake or cupcakes should be refrigerated and not left out longer than 3 hours or frosting will become soft.

Vanilla Frosting

Frosts and Fills a 2 Layer Cake   Veg & V*, Egg Free, Corn Free

- 2 cups **whole** coconut milk, divided: ½ cup + 1½ cups (2 cans needed)
- 2¼ tsp unflavored gelatin
- ¾ cup organic all vegetable shortening such as Spectrum® brand
- ⅓ cup + 1 Tbsp raw honey
- ½ tsp liquid stevia
- 2 tsp vanilla
- ¼ tsp sea salt
- ½ tsp xanthan gum

In a small bowl, whisk together gelatin and ½ cup of milk. In a 2-qt saucepan, on medium heat, warm remaining milk almost to a boil. Remove from heat before boiling. Whisk in gelatin mixture and continue stirring until dissolved. Refrigerate 20 minutes in the pan to cool slightly, stirring occasionally. Put shortening into a blender and add about ⅓ cup of the milk-gelatin mixture. Blend 20 seconds. Continue adding ⅓ cup at a time, blending 20 seconds each time, until all has been added, scraping sides of blender occasionally. Add honey, stevia, vanilla and salt, and blend on low 20 seconds. Scrape sides, add xanthan gum and blend 10 seconds on low, then 40 seconds on high. Scrape sides of blender and blend 20 seconds on high. Pour into a 4 cup container, cover and refrigerate 4-5 hours until firm. Frosted cake or cupcakes should be refrigerated and not left out longer than 3 hours or frosting will become soft.

*Note: For vegetarian or vegan, substitute agar or Veg-a-Gel® for gelatin. Amounts will vary. See Stocking Your GF, DF, SF Pantry, p.6.

"Peanut Butter" Frosting

Frosts and Fills a 2 Layer Cake   Veg & V*, Egg Free, Corn Free

- 2 cups **whole** coconut milk, divided: ½ cup + 1½ cups (2 cans needed)
- 2¼ tsp unflavored gelatin
- ½ cup organic all vegetable shortening such as Spectrum® brand
- ½ cup + 1 Tbsp sunflower seed butter
- ⅓ cup + 1 Tbsp raw honey
- ¾ tsp liquid stevia
- ¼ tsp sea salt
- ½ tsp xanthan gum

Try this frosting on the Chocolate Cake or Cupcakes. Is there a better combo than chocolate and peanut butter? Sprinkle with chopped, toasted almonds for crunch. The almonds actually take on the peanut butter taste.

In a small bowl, whisk together gelatin and ½ cup of milk. In a 2-qt saucepan, on medium heat, warm remaining milk almost to a boil. Remove from heat before boiling. Whisk in gelatin mixture and continue stirring until dissolved. Refrigerate 20 minutes in the pan to cool slightly, stirring occasionally. Put shortening and sunflower seed butter into a blender and add about ⅓ cup of the milk-gelatin mixture. Blend 20 seconds on low. Continue adding ⅓ cup at a time, blending 20 seconds each time, until all has been added, scraping sides of blender occasionally. Add honey, stevia and salt, and blend 20 seconds. Add xanthan gum and blend 10 seconds on low, then scrape sides and blend 40 seconds on high. Pour into a 4 cup container, cover and refrigerate 4-5 hours until firm. Frosted cake or cupcakes should be refrigerated and not left out longer than 3 hours or frosting will become soft.

White Frosting / Coconut Frosting

Frosts and Fills a 2 Layer Cake   Veg & V*, Egg Free, Corn Free

- 2 cups **whole** coconut milk, divided: ½ cup + 1½ cups (2 cans needed)
- 2¼ tsp unflavored gelatin
- ¾ cup organic all vegetable shortening such as Spectrum® brand
- ⅓ cup + 1 Tbsp raw honey
- ½ tsp liquid stevia
- ¼ tsp sea salt
- ½ tsp xanthan gum

For Coconut Frosting

- ¼ cup + ⅓ cup unsweetened medium flaked coconut, like Bob's Red Mill® or Let's Do Organic®

In a small bowl, whisk together gelatin and ½ cup of milk. In a 2-qt saucepan, on medium heat, warm remaining milk almost to a boil. Remove from heat before boiling. Whisk in gelatin mixture and continue stirring until dissolved. Refrigerate 20 minutes in the pan to cool slightly, stirring occasionally. Put shortening into a blender and add about ⅓ cup of the milk-gelatin mixture. Blend 20 seconds on low. Continue adding ⅓ cup at a time, blending 20 seconds each time, until all has been added, scraping sides of blender occasionally. Add honey, stevia and salt, and blend on low 30 seconds. Add xanthan gum and blend 10 seconds on low, then 40 seconds on high. Scrape sides of blender and blend 20 seconds on high. Pour into a 4 cup container, cover and refrigerate 4-5 hours until firm. Frosted cake or cupcakes should be refrigerated and not left out longer than 3 hours or frosting will become soft. For coconut frosting, stir the ¼ cup coconut into frosting before refrigerating. Also, sprinkle the filling layer and top of cake or cupcakes with ⅓ cup shredded coconut immediately after frosting.

*Note: For vegetarian or vegan, substitute agar or Veg-a-Gel® for gelatin. Amounts will vary. See Stocking Your GF, DF, SF Pantry, p.6

Carrot Cake

Makes a 2 Layer Cake Veg, Corn Free

- 4 large eggs
- 2 cups coconut palm sugar
- 1 cup grapeseed oil
- 3 cups shredded carrots
- ½ cup brown rice flour
- ½ cup coconut flour
- ½ cup tapioca flour
- ½ cup potato starch
- 1 tsp baking soda
- 1 tsp aluminum-free, GF baking powder
- ½ tsp sea salt
- ½ tsp xanthan gum
- 1 tsp cinnamon
- ¼ tsp cloves
- • Parchment paper

I was so pleased to arrive at the combination of ingredients to create a moist, light, flavorful carrot cake. Here again, by eating healthy, we're not missing out on anything. This "Cream Cheese" Frosting is delicious and the classic choice for Carrot Cake. If I hadn't mixed it up myself, I wouldn't have believed it is dairy and refined-sugar free.

Trace the bottoms of two 9" cake pans on parchment paper and cut out the rounds of paper. Brush or spray the sides and bottoms of pans and both sides of the parchment paper rounds with grapeseed oil. Sprinkle brown rice flour on cake pan sides and lay a paper round in each pan. In a large mixing bowl, use a standing or hand mixer to beat the eggs. Add the sugar and beat again, scraping the sides of the bowl for 2 minutes. Add the oil and beat until blended. Stir in the carrots. Set aside for at least 10 minutes. Preheat oven to 350°. In another bowl, whisk the flours, potato starch, baking soda, baking powder, salt, xanthan gum, cinnamon and cloves with a wire whisk. Pour the dry ingredients into the egg-carrot mixture a little at a time as you beat until smooth. Pour batter into the pans and bake 25 minutes, or until a toothpick comes out clean. Cool pans on a rack 15 minutes, then turn out cakes on wire racks to cool. Carefully remove parchment paper. Allow cakes to cool completely before frosting. Frost with "Cream Cheese" Frosting.

"Cream Cheese" Frosting

Frosts and Fills a 2 Layer Cake Veg & V (see fn p.141), Egg Free, Corn Free

- 2 cups **whole** coconut milk, divided: ½ cup + 1½ cups (2 cans needed)
- 2¼ tsp unflavored gelatin
- ¾ cup organic all vegetable shortening such as Spectrum® brand
- 2 Tbsp ghee, softened
- ¾ tsp sea salt
- 1½ tsp white vinegar
- ⅓ cup raw honey
- ½ tsp liquid stevia
- ½ tsp xanthan gum

In a small bowl, whisk together the gelatin and ½ cup of the milk. In a 2-qt saucepan, on medium heat, warm the remaining milk almost to a boil. Before boiling, remove from heat. Stir in the milk-gelatin mixture and continue stirring until all of the gelatin is dissolved. Refrigerate 20 minutes in the pan to cool slightly, stirring occasionally. Put the shortening into a blender and add about ⅓ cup of the milk-gelatin mixture. Blend 20 seconds on low speed. Continue adding approximately ⅓ cup at a time followed by blending 20 seconds until all is mixed in, scraping sides of blender occasionally. Add the ghee, salt, vinegar, honey and stevia. Blend 20 seconds on low. Add the xanthan gum and blend 10 seconds on low and then 40 seconds on high. Scrape sides of blender. Blend 20 seconds. Pour into a 4 cup container, cover and refrigerate 4-5 hours or until firm. The frosted cake can be left out for 3 hours but ideally should be refrigerated for longer periods because the frosting will become soft.*

*Times will vary according to the day's temperature.

Chocolate Decadence Pie

Makes a 9" Pie, 12 Servings   Veg, V, Egg Free, Corn Free

Filling

- ⅔ cup plain rice or almond milk
- ¾ cup + 2 Tbsp coconut palm sugar
- 1¼ tsp liquid stevia
- ¼ tsp sea salt
- 1 14 oz package **soft** organic non-GMO tofu
- 8 oz unsweetened baking chocolate (cocoa mass)
- 3 Tbsp sliced almonds, optional

As you savor every bite, consider that you're eating tofu, sugar-free chocolate, whole grain buckwheat and brown rice with natural sweeteners. Serve this to guests and they'll never know it's really "health food." Each slice contains about 6g fiber, 8g protein and only 16g of natural sugar.

Crust

- ¾ cup + 2 Tbsp brown rice flour
- 2 Tbsp tapioca flour
- 1 tsp sea salt
- 1 cup unsweetened cocoa powder
- 1¼ tsp xanthan gum
- 3 Tbsp crushed buckwheat groats
- ½ cup **whole** buckwheat groats such as Pocono® brand*
- ⅓ cup + 1 Tbsp coconut oil
- ¼ cup coconut nectar
- ½ tsp liquid stevia
- 1½ Tbsp water

The secret of this crust is buckwheat. Even though the word "wheat" is in buckwheat, it contains none. The name is misleading because it is not really even a grain, but a fruit that lends some fabulous crunch and nutritious qualities to GF cooking and baking.

Preheat oven to 350°. Brush or spray a 9" pie dish generously with grapeseed oil. In a medium bowl, whisk the flours, salt, cocoa powder and xanthan gum. Into a plastic bag, pour 3 Tbsp of whole buckwheat. Use a rolling pen to crush it into a coarse texture (not powder) and add it to the bowl. Next, add the ½ cup whole buckwheat groats. Use the back of a spoon to thoroughly mix in the oil until it becomes consistently moistened. Then mix in the coconut nectar, stevia and water. Allow to sit 10 minutes to thicken. Turn into pie dish and spread evenly, making the sides no thicker than the bottom. Bake 10 minutes. Cool completely on a rack.

Drain tofu and while it is still in the container, carefully cut it in half. Turn the container and cut in half again so that you have 4 equal quarters. Into a blender, pour the rice milk, sugar, stevia, salt and **only 3 quarters** of the tofu. Blend until smooth. In a double boiler or a 2-qt saucepan sitting atop a smaller pan of simmering water, melt the chocolate. Remove from heat. Turn blender on to lowest speed. Remove lid and pour the melted chocolate into tofu while blending. Use a silicone spatula to scrape in all chocolate. If mixture becomes too thick and blender lags, increase speed slightly. Once all chocolate has been blended in, pour into the pie crust using silicone spatula. Refrigerate 4 hours. Garnish if desired with sliced almonds.

*If you can't find whole buckwheat groats, Pocono® and Bob's Red Mill® make a creamy buckwheat hot cereal that can be substituted, but it won't add as much crunch.

Strawberry "Cream Cheese" Pie

Makes One 10" Pie   Veg & V*, Egg Free, Corn Free

- 1 10" Basic Pie Crust, p.151, baked
- 2¼ tsp unflavored gelatin
- ¼ cup + 1 Tbsp lemon juice
- 2 cups **whole** coconut milk, divided: 1 cup and 1 cup
- ⅓ cup + 1 Tbsp raw honey
- 15 drops liquid stevia
- ¼ tsp sea salt
- 1¼ tsp xanthan gum
- 2 cups strawberries, sliced only ¼ inch thick

If you eat dairy and sugar free, you probably thought you'd never taste a sweet and creamy "cheese" pie again and, if you're gluten free, especially not in a crust. But, once I learned the magic of creative clean cooking, I was, and now you are, able to cook and eat Delightfully Free!

In a small bowl or measuring cup, whisk the gelatin into the lemon juice. In a 2-qt saucepan, stir and warm the first cup of coconut milk on medium heat. Remove from heat right before it boils. Whisk in the lemon-gelatin mixture. Add the raw honey, stevia, salt, and remaining cup of milk, and whisk well. Last, whisk in the xanthan gum until well blended. Refrigerate in the pan about 25 minutes, or just until room temperature, stirring occasionally to keep it from solidifying. Remove from refrigerator. Set aside ⅔ cup of the prettiest sliced strawberries for top. Lay the remaining sliced berries in the bottom of pie crust. Pour the mixture over the berries. Arrange remaining strawberries on top of pie, first dipping each slice in the pie mixture to coat. Carefully place pie uncovered in the refrigerator to chill 2-3 hours until firm, then cover carefully until ready to serve.

*Note: For vegetarian and vegan, substitute agar or Veg-a-Gel® for gelatin. Amounts will vary. See Stocking Your GF, DF, SF Pantry, p.6.

Blueberry Banana Cream Pie

Makes One 10" Pie   Veg*, Corn Free

Crust

- 3 cups unsweetened medium flake coconut**
- ½ cup coconut nectar
- ½ tsp liquid stevia
- ¼ tsp + ⅛ tsp sea salt
- ⅔ cup (about 4 extra large) egg whites, whisked
- 1 tsp vanilla
- 2 Tbsp coconut flour
- ½ tsp xanthan gum

Filling

- 2 tsp unflavored gelatin
- ½ cup whole or light coconut milk, divided: ¼ cup and ¼ cup
- 1⅓ cups **whole** coconut milk
- 4 medium-large bananas + 2 for topping
- 2 heaping Tbsp fresh blueberries + ⅔ cup for topping
- 1 Tbsp vanilla
- ¾ tsp liquid stevia
- 3 Tbsp raw honey
- 2 tsp xanthan gum
- ¼ cup or more lemon juice

Preheat oven to 325°. Spray a 10" pie dish generously with grapeseed oil. In a medium bowl, mix coconut, coconut nectar, stevia and salt. Add egg whites and vanilla. Stir in flour and xanthan gum, and mix well. Allow 5 minutes for mixture to thicken. Turn dough into prepared dish and, using the back of a large spoon, press the mixture evenly into dish, up sides and onto the lip. Bake 18 minutes or until coconut is golden. Cool completely.

In a small bowl, mix gelatin and ¼ cup of milk. Into a blender, pour the 1⅓ cups whole coconut milk, 4 bananas, the 2 Tbsp blueberries, vanilla, stevia and raw honey. Blend until smooth. In a 1-qt saucepan, heat remaining ¼ cup milk on low, and stir in gelatin mixture until it has dissolved. Cool 5 minutes and add it and the xanthan gum to blender. Blend 10 seconds on low. Scrape sides of blender and blend on high 30 seconds. Pour into crust. Refrigerate at least 8 hours to overnight. When pie is completely firm, slice the remaining bananas ¼" thick and swirl them in lemon juice until they are coated. Make a ring of overlapping banana slices around the inside of the crust. Arrange blueberries in the center of pie. Refrigerate until ready to serve. Do not leave pie out of refrigerator for more than an hour or it will become soft.

If you like banana pudding and blueberries, you'll love this summery, cool and creamy dessert. My favorite part is the macaroon crust. This pie is quite eye-catching and makes a perfect dessert for the 4th of July.

* For vegetarian, substitute agar or Veg-a-gel® for gelatin. Amounts will vary. See Stocking Your GF, DF, SF Pantry, p.6.

** If you cannot find medium-flake coconut that is unsweetened, use Bob's Red Mill® or Let's Do Organic® brand which are unsweetened and come in a larger flake. Chop it easily and quickly in a food processor or food chopper to a medium-size flake.

Pumpkin Pie

Makes a 9" Pie

Veg, Corn Free

- 2 extra large eggs
- 1 15 oz can pumpkin
- ½ cup **whole** coconut milk
- ⅓ cup coconut palm sugar
- 3½ Tbsp coconut nectar
- ½ tsp sea salt
- 2 tsp pumpkin pie spice blend
- ¼ tsp + 6 drops liquid stevia
- 1 9" Basic Pie Crust, **unbaked**, recipe is below

Celebrate the holidays with a luscious pumpkin pie. You won't believe how delicious a GF, DF, SF pie can be. If you have extra pumpkin after you have filled the crust, pour it into a ramekin or mini muffin tin which has been brushed with oil. Bake at the same temperature, but for a shorter period of time. Check "pumpkin tarts" after about 15 minutes, depending on size, and remove from oven when they are set just as described in the pie recipe. After cooling 20 minutes, they're wonderful sprinkled with toasted pecans and a scoop of DF ice cream or a dollop of Whipped Topping, p.159.

Preheat oven to 375°. In a medium bowl, whisk eggs. Add remaining ingredients and whisk again until well blended. Pour mixture into **unbaked** pie crust. Do not overfill. (see above for what to do with any extra pumpkin filling). Place pie in center of oven and bake 10 minutes at 375°. Turn heat down to 325° and continue baking 35-40 minutes. Use a pie crust shield for the last 10 minutes if crust is becoming too brown. The filling will be set, but center of filling will still be soft when done. Cool completely on a rack before serving.

Basic Pie Crust

Makes a 9" Crust or a 10" Crust

Veg, V, Egg Free, Corn Free

9 Inch Crust

- 1½ cups brown rice flour
- ¼ cup tapioca flour
- 1¹⁄₁₆ tsp sea salt
- ½ tsp + ⅛ tsp cinnamon
- 1 tsp xanthan gum
- ⅓ cup + 1 Tbsp coconut oil, softened
- 3 Tbsp coconut nectar
- 6 drops liquid stevia
- 2 tsp water

10 Inch Crust

- 2 cups brown rice flour
- ⅓ cup tapioca flour
- 1⅓ tsp sea salt
- 1 tsp cinnamon
- 1⅓ tsp xanthan gum
- ½ cup + 1½ tsp coconut oil, softened
- ¼ cup coconut nectar
- 8 drops liquid stevia
- 2½ tsp water

No need to roll this crust. It is quick and easy to make and tastes like the wonderful pie crusts we fondly remember and miss like crazy!

Preheat oven to 350°. Brush or spray a 9 or 10" pie dish with grapeseed oil. In a medium bowl, whisk flours, salt, cinnamon and xanthan gum together. Add the coconut oil. Mix well, using a large spoon, taking time to press and stir dough until it becomes consistently moistened. Add the coconut nectar, stevia and water. Stir until well combined. Turn dough into the prepared pie dish and, using your hands or the back of a spoon, bring it all the way up the sides and onto the lip of the dish. If pre-baking the crust before filling it, bake crust 14-16 minutes, until light golden. Cool completely on a rack.

Orange Cranberry Crumble

Makes 8-10 Servings   Veg, V, Egg Free, Corn Free

Filling

- 6 cups fresh or frozen cranberries, washed & sorted
- 1 cup fresh grated orange zest, about 2½ large oranges
- ½ cup fresh squeezed orange juice
- 4 cups green apples, peeled, cored and sliced thin, about 4 apples
- 2 Tbsp tapioca flour
- 1¼ cups coconut palm sugar
- 1 tsp liquid stevia

In a 4-qt saucepan, bring cranberries, orange zest, orange juice and apples to a boil. Turn heat down to medium and cook 10 minutes until most of the cranberries have popped. Reduce heat to low and stir in the tapioca flour. Stir 1 minute until the juices thicken. Remove from heat and stir in the sugar and 1 tsp stevia.

Crust and Topping

- 3 cups almond meal
- 1½ cups creamy buckwheat cereal, such as Bob's Red Mill® or Pocono®
- 1⅛ tsp sea salt
- 1½ cups finely chopped walnuts
- ⅓ cup + 2 Tbsp grapeseed oil
- ⅓ cup + 2 Tbsp coconut nectar
- 1 tsp liquid stevia

Preheat oven to 350°. Brush or spray a 9x13 baking dish with grapeseed oil. In a large bowl, stir together the almond meal, buckwheat, salt and nuts. In a small bowl, whisk the oil, coconut nectar and 1 tsp stevia. Stir into the dry mixture until crumbly. Press about ⅔ of the crumble mixture into bottom of baking dish using the flat of your hand. Spread the cranberry mixture over crust. Spoon remaining crumble mixture over the filling. Place in the oven and lay a baking sheet on top to cover while baking. Bake 40 minutes. Remove the baking-sheet cover, and bake another 5 minutes or until filling is beginning to bubble and the topping is golden brown.

Mouth watering, tart & sweet with a warm nutty crumble. Enjoy it with the Whipped Topping, p.159 or DF vanilla ice cream.

I don't use aluminum foil in baking or cooking because of the possible transfer of aluminum to the food. A baking sheet works just as well.

Rhubarb or Peach Crumble

Serves 6 Veg, V, Egg Free, Corn Free

The rhubarb version is tart and the peach version is sweet. Both are as scrumptious as they are healthy.

Crust and Topping

- ¾ cup coconut oil
- ¾ cup coconut palm sugar
- 1 tsp vanilla
- ¾ tsp liquid stevia
- 2 Tbsp flaxseed meal
- ½ tsp xanthan gum
- 1 tsp sea salt
- ½ cup brown rice flour
- ½ cup tapioca flour
- 1¼ cups quinoa flakes, such as Ancient Harvest® brand
- 1 cup chopped toasted walnuts
- 1 cup chopped toasted almonds

Rhubarb Filling

- 24 oz fresh or frozen rhubarb (frozen works best), defrosted, sliced into 1" lengths
- ½ cup coconut nectar, to taste
- 1 Tbsp tapioca flour
- ½ tsp + ⅛ tsp liquid stevia

In a 3-qt saucepan over medium heat, bring rhubarb to a simmer and stir about 3 minutes to extract the juices, just until rhubarb is al dente. Remove from heat and stir in the coconut nectar and stevia. Stir in the tapioca flour. Simmer 1 minute, stirring until the juices thicken. Remove from heat.

Peach Filling

- 2¼ lb ripe peaches, about 4½ cups, peeled and sliced
- 2-3 Tbsp coconut nectar, depending on the sweetness of the peaches
- ¼ tsp cinnamon
- ¼ tsp sea salt
- ¼ tsp liquid stevia, only if needed

In a large bowl, toss the peaches with remaining ingredients until coated and set aside.

To toast nuts, preheat oven to 350°. Spread nuts on a baking sheet and bake about 5 minutes, until light golden and fragrant.

Preheat oven to 350°. Brush or spray an 8x11 pan with grapeseed oil. In a medium bowl, stir together the oil and sugar. Add the vanilla, stevia and flaxseed meal. Mix in the xanthan gum, salt and the 2 flours. Add the quinoa flakes and both nuts, and toss until crumbly. Press ½ of the mixture into the bottom of pan. Pour filling on top. Cover with remaining crumble mixture. Bake 30 minutes until the top is golden brown and the edges are slightly bubbly. Cool on a wire rack 15 minutes.

Desserts & Candy

Chocolate Mousse

Serves 4 Veg, V, Egg Free, Corn Free

- 1 13½ oz can Thai Kitchen® **whole** coconut milk*
- ⅓ cup coconut palm sugar
- ⅛+1/16 tsp sea salt
- ½ tsp xanthan gum
- 2½ Tbsp unsweetened cocoa powder
- 12-14 drops liquid stevia**

Sweet and creamy! Quick to prepare, but fancy when served in a stemmed glass and sprinkled with chocolate shavings. Spoon it into a kid-safe bowl and even a DF, SF toddler can enjoy it!

* I have tried other brands of coconut milk for this recipe, but Thai Kitchen® brand is the only one I find to be creamy enough to work.

** Be careful when you add the stevia. It is extremely sweet and it's easy to use too much, so add only 4-5 drops at a time and taste.

Into a blender, pour the milk, sugar, salt, xanthan gum, cocoa powder and 12 to 14 drops of stevia. Use the lowest speed on blender, such as "stir," for 10 seconds. Scrape the sides of the blender and blend on a higher speed 40 seconds. Pour into a 2 cup container or individual serving bowls, cover and chill for 2 hours. It will continue to thicken as it chills.

Coconut Tapioca Pudding

Serves 4-6 Veg, V, Egg Free, Corn Free

- ½ cup tapioca small pearls in 1 cup of water
- 2½ cups water
- ¾ tsp sea salt
- ¾ cup coconut palm sugar
- ¾ tsp liquid stevia
- 1-1½ cups fresh coconut meat, chopped into ⅓" pieces, or a 15 oz can coconut meat, drained and cut into ⅓" pieces

Coconut Sauce

- 1 14 oz can **whole** coconut milk
- ½ tsp liquid stevia
- ½ tsp sea salt, to taste
- • ground cinnamon

Soak the tapioca pearls in 1 cup water 15-20 minutes. Meanwhile, pour 2½ cups water and the salt into a 2-qt saucepan. Drain pearls and add them to the saucepan. Turn heat to medium-high and bring to a boil, stirring occasionally. Once it boils, turn heat to medium-low and simmer 6-8 minutes or until tapioca becomes translucent and thickens. Add coconut sugar, stirring until it has dissolved. Remove from heat and stir in the stevia and coconut meat. Set aside. Combine all sauce ingredients in a 1-qt saucepan. Cook on medium heat, stirring until heated. The sauce will not thicken. To serve, spoon the warm tapioca pudding into serving bowls and pour a generous amount of the sauce on top. Garnish with a sprinkle of cinnamon.

This simple dessert is sweet and exotic. It consists mainly of coconut, an amazing food. One cup of coconut meat has 7.2g fiber, and more than half the recommended daily amount of manganese, which helps metabolize fat and proteins, supports the immune and nervous systems, and promotes stable blood sugar levels. One cup of coconut milk has 38.4mg calcium, around 89mg magnesium (which helps maintain normal blood pressure, lowering the risk of heart disease), and is an excellent source of potassium (631mg) and phosphorus (240mg). It helps increase energy levels and promotes bone and kidney health. Try this dessert with Thai Coconut Chicken or Grilled Basil Shrimp & Chicken.

Eggnog Bread Pudding with Rum Sauce

Serves 8-10 **Veg, Corn Free**

- 6 large eggs
- 1¾ cups coconut palm sugar
- 2 tsp nutmeg
- 3 tsp cinnamon
- 2 tsp vanilla
- 1½ tsp liquid stevia
- 1½ cups vanilla rice milk
- 1½ cups **whole** coconut milk
- 10 cups 1" cubes GF bread such as EnerG® or Glutino® brown rice breads
- 1 cup golden raisins

Rum Sauce

- 2 cups water
- 1 cup coconut palm sugar
- 2 Tbsp tapioca flour
- ⅓ cup white rum, or more to taste
- ¼ tsp sea salt
- ⅓ cup **whole** coconut milk

Another dessert that seems like an impossibility for GF, DF, SF eaters. But this warm, cinnamon sweet bread pudding, complete with traditional rum sauce, is, in fact, legit and legal! Especially nice for the holidays or for a large gathering.

Preheat oven to 325°. Spray a 9x13 baking dish with grapeseed oil. In a large bowl, whisk eggs. Add sugar, nutmeg, cinnamon, vanilla and stevia, and whisk again. Whisk in rice and coconut milks. Add bread cubes and raisins. Stir until well combined and bread is soaked with liquid. Pour the mixture into baking dish and bake 55 minutes or until a knife inserted in center comes out clean. Serve warm with rum sauce.

For sauce, in a 2-qt saucepan, heat water and sugar on medium-high, stirring occasionally, until it comes to a boil. Lower heat and simmer 5 minutes. Remove from heat. Cool to lukewarm. Whisk in tapioca flour. Return to medium heat. Stirring constantly, bring to a low boil and continue to cook and stir 1 minute. Remove from heat and cool again to lukewarm. Whisk in rum, salt and coconut milk.

Whipped Topping

Makes 2 Cups **Veg, V, Egg Free, Corn Free**

- 1 13½ or 14 oz can **whole** coconut milk
- 15 drops liquid stevia*
- • less than 1/16 tsp sea salt
- ½ tsp xanthan gum

optional: 2 tsp coconut nectar (which if used will tint whipped topping a shade darker)

What a treat! This seems to defy the DF, SF rule, yet is surprisingly Delightfully Free. The perfect touch to complement Pumpkin Pie, Chocolate Decadence Pie, crumble recipes, the Mousse or anything enhanced by whipped cream.

Into a blender, pour the milk, only 15 drops of stevia*, salt, xanthan gum and the coconut nectar if using. Use the lowest speed on blender, such as "stir," 10 seconds. Scrape the sides of blender and blend on a higher speed 40 seconds. Pour into a 2 cup container with a lid and chill for 2 hours. It will continue to thicken as it chills.

*Be careful adding the stevia. It is very sweet and can overpower this delicate topping. Add only 4-5 drops at a time and taste.

Dark Chocolate Hearts

Makes about 2½ Cups **Veg, V, Egg Free, Corn Free**

- 8 oz unsweetened baking chocolate (cocoa mass)
- ½ cup + 1 Tbsp coconut nectar
- 1¾ tsp liquid stevia for dark chocolate lovers*
- 3 Tbsp **whole** coconut milk
- ¼ tsp sea salt
- • heart-shaped mold**

Rich and flavorful as those from fancy stores, yet guilt-free, these chocolatey hearts are perfect for those who limit sugar. Pair them with Dark Chocolate Truffles for a beautiful array of confections.

**Heart shaped molds made of tin, plastic or silicone are available in most kitchen or craft stores.

It is best to have all ingredients measured out before beginning. Brush the heart mold lightly with grapeseed oil. In a double boiler or a 2-qt pan over a smaller pan of simmering water, melt the chocolate. Remove from heat. Stir in the reamining ingredients. Gently press chocolate mixture into each heart mold with fingers, causing it to take the heart shape, eliminating bubbles and making the tops even. Chill in the refrigerator 2 hours or until chocolate hearts are hardened. Remove from mold and enjoy! Store in an air-tight container in refrigerator.

Dark Chocolate Truffles

Makes 18 1½" Truffles **Veg, V, Egg Free, Corn Free**

- 8 oz unsweetened baking chocolate (cocoa mass)
- ½ cup + 1 Tbsp coconut nectar
- 1¾ tsp liquid stevia for dark chocolate lovers*
- 3 Tbsp **whole** coconut milk
- ¼ tsp sea salt
- ½ cup chopped toasted almonds or hazelnuts, optional

Optional Coatings

- ½ cup finely ground, toasted almonds or hazelnuts with a pinch of sea salt
- 3-4 Tbsp unsweetened cocoa powder

I never dreamed it could be so easy to create such a fancy, sophisticated indulgence. And the biggest surprise is that each truffle has only about 6.7g natural, unrefined sugar.

It is best to have all ingredients measured out before beginning. In a double boiler or a 2-qt saucepan over a smaller pan of simmering water, melt the chocolate. Remove from heat. Stir in the remaining ingredients. Mix in the ½ cup chopped nuts, if desired, and form 1½" balls by rolling the chocolate in your hands. If using the optional ground nuts or powdered chocolate, pour your choice on a sheet of wax paper and roll each truffle in it. Place each completed truffle on a wax paper-lined tray or baking sheet. Chill in the refrigerator 2 hours or until hardened. For softer truffles, allow them to sit out of the fridge a few minutes before serving. Enjoy! Store truffles in an air-tight container in refrigerator.

* If you like your chocolate a little sweeter, add ¼ tsp more stevia and/or a tsp more coconut nectar.

Healthy Hot Cocoa

Serves 2 **Veg, V, Egg Free, Corn Free**

2 cups vanilla rice or almond milk
1 Tbsp unsweetened cocoa powder
1 Tbsp + 1 tsp coconut palm sugar

Hot cocoa is that special treat we look forward to when coming in from the cold or to share on a family game night. Now, even if we are DF and SF, we can still enjoy a chocolatey sweet mug of Hot Cocoa with a cookie or some chocolate pretzels.

In a saucepan, warm the milk. Stir in the remaining ingredients. Easy to double or triple the servings if you have more cocoa drinkers, or to halve for just one. To make even richer, substitute some of the milk with coconut milk.

Dark Chocolate Covered Pretzels

Makes 3½ Cups **Veg, V, Egg Free, Corn Free**

4 oz or about 3½ cups GF pretzels such as EnerG® or Glutino®
cup DF chocolate chips (see suggested chocolates on p.7)

Lay a sheet of wax paper out on the counter. Melt the chocolate chips in a double boiler over simmering water. Stir the pretzels into the chocolate and then place each pretzel on the wax paper spaced apart so they are not touching. Allow chocolate to harden either at room temperature or more quickly in the refrigerator.

Tracy's Delights

Makes 25 Squares **Veg, V, Egg Free, Corn Free**

1 cup coarsely chopped toasted almonds
2 cups 100% crispy brown rice, divided
¾ cup coconut nectar
1½ tsp liquid stevia
¼ tsp + ⅛ tsp sea salt
¾ cup sunflower seed butter
6 oz unsweetened baking chocolate
¼ cup + 2 Tbsp Enjoy Life® Crunchy Flax cereal **or** additional chopped toasted almonds

Chocolate & peanut butter is a fabulous combination! But, because peanuts raise allergy and inflammation concerns, I use sunflower seed butter which is also creamy, rich and tastes like peanut butter. Add some crispy crunch, and you have my surprisingly nutritious Tracy's Delights.

Spray an 8x8 pan generously with grapeseed oil. Pour almonds evenly into the bottom. Sprinkle only ½ cup of the rice over top. Set aside the remaining 1½ cups rice and flax cereal in a bowl. Measure out coconut nectar. Stir into it the stevia and salt. Measure sunflower seed butter and set aside. In a double boiler or a 2-qt saucepan over a smaller pan of simmering water, melt chocolate. Remove from heat and stir in sunflower seed butter. Next, mix in rice-cereal mixture until well coated. Add coconut nectar-stevia-salt, stir well and spoon into pan. Spread to the edges and press down gently. Cover and refrigerate 2 hours. Cut into 1½" squares and enjoy!

Jesus said to them, “I am the bread of life; whoever comes to Me shall not hunger, and whoever believes in Me shall never thirst.” John 6:35

Index

a

B

C

D

E

F

G

H

I

S

T

V

W

X

Y

Z